Gateway

Workbook

2nd Edition

David Spencer
Lynda Edwards

B1

Contents B1

		Vocabulary / Developing vocabulary	Reading	Grammar
Unit 1	**Family life** p4	Ages and stages of life, The family p4 Noun suffixes -ment, -ion, -ence p7	A blog about teenage problems p5	Present simple and present continuous p6 Articles p8
Unit 2	**Who did it?** p12	Crime and criminals, Detective work p12 Phrasal verbs connected with investigating and finding p15	Detectives with a difference p13	Past simple p14 Past continuous p16
✓ Gateway to exams: Units 1–2 p20				
Unit 3	**Universal language** p22	Countries and nationalities, Learning a language p22 Negative prefixes un-, in-, im-, ir-, il- p25	A dead language p23	some, any, much, many, a lot (of), a few, a little p24 Relative pronouns p26
Unit 4	**Health watch** p30	Parts of the body, Health problems and illnesses p30 Compound nouns connected with health and medicine p33	A blog about a health problem p31	Present perfect with ever, never, for and since p32 Present perfect with just, yet and already p34
✓ Gateway to exams: Units 3–4 p38				
Unit 5	**TV addicts** p40	Television, Adjectives describing TV programmes p40 Adjectives ending in -ing and -ed p43	The way forward p41	Comparative and superlatives p42 less … than, (not) as … as, too and (not) enough p44
Unit 6	**Planet Earth** p48	Geographical features, The environment p48 Different uses of get p51	The world's most expensive burger p49	be going to, will, may, might p50 Zero and first conditionals p52
✓ Gateway to exams: Units 5–6 p56				
Unit 7	**Job hunting** p58	Jobs and work, Personal qualities p58 Compound adjectives p61	A smelly job p59	Modal verbs of obligation, prohibition and advice p60 Second conditional p62
Unit 8	**Best friends forever** p66	Friendships, Feelings p66 Noun suffixes -ness, -ship, -dom p69	Best friends forever?? p67	Past perfect, used to p68 Gerunds and infinitives p70
✓ Gateway to exams: Units 7–8 p74				
Unit 9	**Bestsellers** p76	Fiction, Non-fiction p76 Phrasal verbs connected with reading and writing p79	The cell phone novel p77	Reported speech – statements p78 Reported speech – questions p80
Unit 10	**Log on** p84	Using a computer, The Internet p84 Collocations with email p87	Crime or hobby? p85	The passive – present simple p86 The passive – other tenses p88
✓ Gateway to exams: Units 9–10 p92				

Study skills   p94

Listening	Speaking	Writing	Study skills
Family life **p7**	Asking for personal information **p9**	An informal email **p10**	Grammar: Using reference material **p6** Writing: Keeping a mistakes checklist **p10**
Detective stories **p15**	Apologising **p17**	A blog post **p18**	Vocabulary: Using a dictionary **p12** Reading: Prediction **p13**
Jobs **p25**	Asking for information **p27**	A language biography **p28**	Knowing what type of learner you are **p22** Listening: Keeping calm **p25**
A hospital TV drama **p33**	Describing photos **p35**	Notes and messages **p36**	Keeping vocabulary records **p30** Speaking: Words you don't know **p35**
Events and feelings **p43**	Negotiating **p45**	A review **p46**	Reading for general information **p41** Grammar: Use and form **p44**
Climate change **p51**	Making arrangements **p53**	A formal letter **p54**	First listening, second listening **p51** Organising ideas into paragraphs **p54**
University **p61**	Making polite requests **p63**	A letter of application and CV **p64**	Efficient vocabulary revision **p61** Speaking: Making mistakes **p63**
A best friend **p69**	Reporting a past event **p71**	An email of advice **p72**	Reading for specific information **p67** Listening outside the classroom **p69**
Reading and writing **p79**	A presentation **p81**	A story **p82**	Reading for pleasure **p77** Practising your writing **p82**
Problems with emails **p87**	Comparing and contrasting photos **p89**	Text messages **p90**	Reading: Guessing from context **p85** Speaking: Practice makes perfect **p89**

1 Family Life

Vocabulary

1 Read the clues on the right and complete the puzzle. Which word appears in the shaded column?

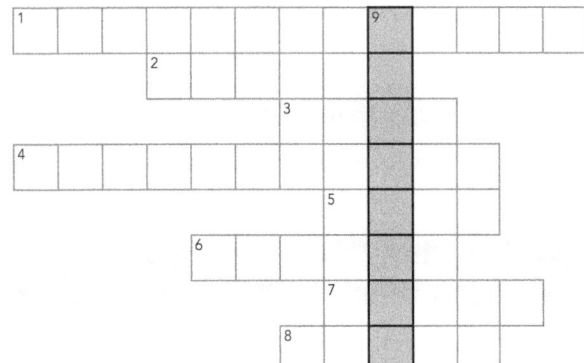

1 He's 72. He's a ....
2 & 3 She's 55. She's a .... woman.
4 the period of life when you change from being a child to being a young adult
5 a very young child who can't talk or walk
6 the stage of life when you are 70, for example
7 the opposite of life
8 the beginning of life
9 ....

2 Use words from the puzzle to complete the sentences.

1 We're celebrating the .... of our new sister.
2 I was very sad at the .... of my aunt.
3 .... is a difficult time for many people. They aren't children, but they aren't adults either.
4 When you're sitting on the bus, you should always offer your seat to a ....
5 It's important to look after your parents in their ....

4 Match the halves to make sentences.

1 I've got a stepfather because
2 My aunt is 50 and single because
3 She's my niece because
4 Paul is an only child because
5 I come from a one-parent family because
6 Peter is my cousin's partner, not her husband, because
7 Samuel is divorced because

a his parents didn't want any more children.
b they don't want to get married at the moment.
c my parents got divorced and I live with my mum.
d my mum got married again.
e she's my sister Elizabeth's daughter.
f he separated from his wife legally last year.
g she never wants to get married.

3 Complete the sentences.

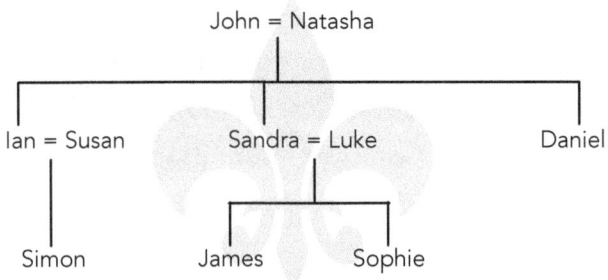

1 John and Natasha are Simon's *grandparents* .
2 Susan is Ian's ....
3 James is Simon's ....
4 Natasha is Luke's ....
5 Luke is Ian's ....
6 Daniel is Simon's ....
7 Sophie is Ian's ....
8 James is Daniel's ....
9 Sophie is John's ....
10 Luke is Sandra's ....

VOCABULARY EXTENSION

5 Complete the definitions with the words in the box.

| graduate • infant • orphan • pensioner |
| toddler • tween • twin |

1 A .... has a sister or brother with the same birth date.
2 An .... is a child with no parents.
3 When you finish university you are a ....
4 After you retire, you become a .... and get money from the government.
5 A .... is a child between two and four.
6 An .... is a child in its first year.
7 A .... is a child who is not yet a teenager (about 10–12 years old).

4 Unit 1 I can talk about stages of life and families

Reading

1 Look at the photo. Why do you think Ella is angry with her sister? Read the blog quickly to check your answer.

a because she shares the same room
b because she never leaves her alone
c because she borrows her clothes

Ella's blog

BLOG   ABOUT ME   SEARCH

Hi everyone!
Generally speaking I'm enjoying life as a teenager, but there are times when it really gets me down. It's great that my parents are giving me a bit more independence. I have a really good group of friends and I see them two or three times a week. We go swimming every weekend, too. That's the good part. But one part of my life is definitely getting worse – and that's my relationship with my younger sister, Hanna. It is becoming an absolute nightmare. She's two years younger than me, but she wants to do exactly the same things as I do. That means she wants to have the same hairstyle as I have, she copies my clothes, she even wears the same make-up as me. And sometimes she makes me furious because she borrows my clothes without asking. I hate it. In fact, while I'm writing this blog I can see her from my room. She's in the back garden and she's wearing my white T-shirt and jeans, which are now really dirty because she's lying on her back in the grass. My parents know about this because I always tell them, but they don't understand. They think it's fine. They say my sister's younger than me so I need to be kind to her. But they're my clothes and it's my room. It's private!
I also have an older brother, Jimmy, who is really great. He goes to a different school because he's older, but he always helps me with my homework if it's difficult. My laptop sometimes breaks and he repairs it for me. He loves playing computer games and he often lets me play, too. We get on very well. Hanna never goes into his room or takes his things. I know she doesn't want his clothes. But she doesn't even go in there to borrow a pen or some paper – or play a computer game while he's out. Why me???

2 **Read the blog again and choose the best answers.**

1 Ella is quite happy at the moment because …
  a she's got more freedom than before.
  b she likes going out with her family.
  c she's getting on well with her school work.
2 Ella's sister wants …
  a to use Ella's laptop all the time.
  b to look just like Ella.
  c to copy all Ella's work.
3 Ella gets angry because …
  a her parents always agree with her sister.
  b she has to share a room with her sister.
  c her parents don't buy her new clothes.
4 Ella's brother is …
  a unkind to her sister.
  b good with computers.
  c away at university a lot.
5 Which would be the best title for the blog?
  a My brother's amazing!
  b My parents don't understand me!
  c My sister's annoying!

3 **CRITICAL THINKING**

Which of these statements are good (G) and which bad (B) advice for Ella?

1 Shout at your sister so she doesn't do it again.   G / B
2 Borrow some of her clothes and throw them away.   G / B
3 Tell your parents every time she takes something.   G / B
4 Talk to her and say she can borrow some things, but not others.   G / B
5 Put a lock on your door so no one can go in.   G / B
6 Give her some of your old clothes.   G / B
7 Offer her style advice.   G / B

4 **Match the underlined words in the blog with the definitions.**

1 makes me upset ....
2 very angry ....
3 a big problem ....
4 uses something that belongs to someone else, then gives it back later ....
5 fixes something broken ....

5 **Complete the sentences with the correct form of the words or phrases from 4.**

1 If I get bad results in a test, it ....
2 I've got to rewrite an essay for the teacher. It's an ....
3 My mum was .... when Dad crashed her car.
4 When I dropped my mobile phone on the floor, it was impossible to .... it.
5 I don't like to .... money from friends.

I can understand a blog about teenage problems   Unit 1   5

Grammar in context

1 Read the uses (a–d) for the present simple and present continuous. Decide if they are uses for the present simple (S) or present continuous (C).

a actions that are happening now or temporary situations   S / C
b regular habits and routines   S / C
c things that are generally true   S / C
d with verbs like *love, hate, know, understand*   S / C

2 Match the sentences with the uses from 1.

1 She's lying on the grass at the moment. ....
2 My laptop sometimes breaks. ....
3 I see my friends three times a week. ....
4 She makes me furious. ....
5 She's wearing my T-shirt and jeans. ....
6 I have a really good group of friends. ....
7 He loves playing computer games. ....
8 We go swimming every weekend. ....

STUDY SKILLS

When you have a problem with grammar, where can you find help?

➤ STUDY SKILLS page 94

3 Complete the dialogues with the present simple or the present continuous form of the verbs given.

1 A: Why has he got his hand up?
   B: He .... (want) the teacher to ask him. He .... (know) the answer.

2 A: Why .... you .... (study)?
   B: I've got an exam tomorrow.

3 A: How do you prepare for exams?
   B: I .... (read) my notes and then I .... (write) questions for myself.

4 A: Who .... (sing) downstairs?
   B: That's my sister. She's good, isn't she?

5 A: *Bonjour, Mademoiselle.*
   B: Sorry, I .... (not speak) French.

6 A: What's that smell? Is it pizza?
   B: Yes. My dad .... (cook) dinner.

7 A: Why isn't your mum here at the moment?
   B: She .... (finish) work late on Thursdays.

8 A: Can I speak to the director?
   B: No. He .... (speak) to someone.

4 Write questions using the prompts below.

1 Where/you/live?
   Where do you live?
2 Where/your mother/work?
   ....
3 you/have/a best friend/at the moment?
   ....
4 your friend/speak English/well?
   ....
5 you/do/your homework/at the moment?
   ....
6 What/sports/you/do?
   ....
7 What/your friend/read/at the moment?
   ....
8 Who/you/usually/sit next to/in English lessons?
   ....

GRAMMAR CHALLENGE

5 Find and correct the mistakes. Two of the sentences are correct.

1 Are you writting your essay at the moment?
2 She doesn't have her books with her today?
3 Do you studying for your exam now?
4 Why are you and Joe walking to school today?
5 Do your brother plays in the basketball team?
6 My cousin studies at this school.
7 My sister and I are having two bikes at the moment.
8 A: What do you do now?
   B: I listen to my MP3 player.
9 Does your parents work at the hospital?
10 I am loving listening to music.

---

6   Unit 1   I can talk about life using the present simple and present continuous

Developing vocabulary and listening

1 **Write the noun form of these words.**
   1 concentrate (v) ....
   2 describe (v) ....
   3 argue (v) ....
   4 independent (adj) ....
   5 discuss (v) ....
   6 improve (v) ....
   7 retire (v) ....
   8 move (v) ....
   9 adolescent (adj) ....
   10 inform (v) ....
   11 different (adj) ....
   12 confident (adj) ....

2 **Match some of the words in 1 with the definitions. Write the correct form of the word.**
   1 facts about someone or something ....
   2 make something better ....
   3 something that makes one thing not the same as another ....
   4 a bad disagreement with someone ....
   5 talk about something with others ....
   6 young, growing into an adult ....

3 **LISTENING** ▶ 01 **Listen to the speakers. What change in someone's life are they talking about?**
   a moving to a different town
   b moving away from home
   c moving to another country

4 ▶ 01 **Listen to the speakers again. Match each person (1–4) to a statement (a–h).**
   1 Anna ☐ ☐
   2 Ethan ☐ ☐
   3 Alex ☐ ☐
   4 Grace ☐ ☐

   a sees their parents regularly
   b lives closer to their friends now
   c would prefer a bigger place
   d doesn't get so tired now
   e does better work now
   f doesn't like housework
   g works in the evening
   h has a big family

⊕ VOCABULARY EXTENSION

5 **We can add the suffixes -er, -or, -ist to verbs or nouns to make nouns that describe people. We usually add -er and -or to verbs and -ist to nouns. Write the nouns for these words. Use your dictionary if necessary.**
   1 art *artist*
   2 sing ....
   3 drive ....
   4 invent ....
   5 science ....
   6 economy ....
   7 teach ....
   8 play ....
   9 photograph ....
   10 direct ....
   11 write ....
   12 build ....

6 **Complete the sentences with the words from 5.**
   1 He always wins at tennis. He's a very good ....
   2 Steven Spielberg is a very famous film ....
   3 Albert Einstein was a great ....
   4 Is your dad a taxi ....?
   5 I hate that .... All her songs are the same.
   6 I'd like to be an .... one day. I love studying finance and markets.
   7 It was his job to create new things. He was an ....
   8 She asks us lots of questions. She's a really good ....
   9 I like that .... He takes really good photographs.
   10 He writes really good books for teenagers. He's a ....
   11 He's my favourite .... He paints beautiful pictures of the countryside.
   12 I called a .... when there was a problem with the roof of my house.

Grammar in context

1 Complete the sentences with the correct article.

> a/an • a/an • 0 (no article) • the • the

1. Now I live in .... flat.
2. I was having a lot of arguments with my parents about .... politics.
3. I'm .... restaurant manager.
4. .... flat's a bit small.
5. I recently moved into my own flat near .... beach.

2 Match the rules with the sentences from 1.

a. We use no article when we talk about things in general. ....
b. We use *the* to talk about a specific person or thing or previously mentioned person or thing. ....
c. We use *a/an* to talk about a singular, countable person or thing for the first time, or to say that the person or thing is one of a number of people or things. ....
d. We use *the* to talk about someone or something that is unique. ....
e. We use *a/an* to say what somebody's profession is. ....

3 Complete the sentences with *a/an* or *the*.

1. .... teacher in the photo looks very clever.
2. My brother has got .... new mobile phone!
3. What's .... title of that song?
4. He works for .... organisation that helps people.
5. .... boy behind you is Paul's cousin.
6. What's on TV? Can you pass .... remote control?
7. She's single. She hasn't got .... husband.
8. I have .... idea! Why don't we go out tomorrow?
9. Alex is .... name of my nephew.
10. My stepfather is .... builder.
11. He is .... director of the film we saw yesterday.
12. My sister wants to be .... economist.
13. Have you got .... new hat? I haven't seen it before.
14. .... coat you are wearing looks very warm.

4 Complete the famous quotes with *a/an*, *the* or *0* (no article).

1. 'I have .... dream.' *Martin Luther King*
2. '........ Earth goes round .... Sun.' *Copernicus*
3. 'I paint .... objects as I think them, not as I see them.' *Pablo Picasso*
4. 'To be or not to be, that is .... question.' *William Shakespeare*
5. '........ Imagination/imagination is more important than .... knowledge.' *Albert Einstein*
6. 'Nothing is more responsible for .... good old days than .... bad memory.' *Franklin Pierce Adams*
7. '........ Only/only problem with common sense is that it is not very common.' *Voltaire*
8. '........ Life/life is a dream.' *Calderón de la Barca*

⊕ GRAMMAR CHALLENGE

5 Cross out the extra word in the sentences.

1. I love the Italian food.
2. The English people I am know are really nice.
3. We are go to the shopping centre on Saturdays.
4. All you need is the love.
5. Is the food in this restaurant is good?
6. Does your brother is enjoy pop music?
7. Where do are you going now?
8. The vegetarians don't eat meat.
9. We don't not like the new restaurant.

Unit 1 **I can use articles**

Developing speaking

1 **LISTENING** ▶ 02 **Listen to the dialogue. Tick (✓) the correct information.**
   1 The girl's name is Marie. ☐
   2 The girl has two sisters. ☐
   3 She sees her sister, Jenny, every month. ☐
   4 The girl usually does her homework with a friend. ☐
   5 The boy plays a lot of computer games. ☐
   6 The girl watches films on television. ☐

2 **Put the words in order to find questions from the dialogue. Add question marks.**
   ☐ 1 your what's name
   ....
   ☐ 2 often you how see them do
   ....
   ☐ 3 like games computer you do
   ....
   ☐ 4 any you sisters got or brothers have
   ....
   ☐ 5 they school to do your go
   ....
   ☐ 6 you what evenings in do the do
   ....

3 ▶ 02 **Put the questions from 2 in the order the boy asks them in the dialogue. Listen and check.**

4 **Complete the dialogue with the correct questions (a–g).**
   a Do you like swimming?
   b Are you a new student?
   c What do you think of the shops in town?
   d How often do you go swimming?
   e Do they go to this school, too?
   f What do you do at weekends?
   g Have you got any brothers or sisters?

   A: Hi! I'm Sofie.
   B: I'm Edward. **(1)** ....
   A: Yes, I am. I'm starting today with my brother.
      (2) ....
   B: Yes, I've got two brothers.
   A: **(3)** ....
   B: Yes. But they're not in my class, thank goodness!
   A: I've joined the swimming club.
      (4) ....
   B: Not really. I prefer football.
      (5) ....
   A: At the moment, I go twice a week in the evenings.
   B: **(6)** ....
   A: I usually just go shopping with my mates.
   B: **(7)** ....
   A: They're really good and not too expensive.

💬 PRONUNCIATION

5 ▶ 03 **Read the questions and underline the words you think are stressed. Listen and check.**
   1 What do you do?
   2 Where do you live?
   3 What sports do you like?
   4 Where does your dad work?
   5 How do you travel to school?

➕ DESCRIBING PICTURES

6 **Look at the photo and write your answers to the questions in your notebook. If you're not sure of something, use *I think* and/or *I imagine*.**

   1 Who can you see in the picture?
   2 Where are they?
   3 What are they doing?
   4 How do you think they are feeling? Why?

7 **LISTENING** ▶ 04 **Listen to a student talking about the photo. What are her answers to the questions?**

8 **SPEAKING** **Now look at the second photo and answer the same questions.**

I can ask for personal information Unit 1 9

Developing writing

1 Read this student's paragraph plan and email. Then put the email in the order of the paragraph plan.

Paragraph plan
Informal email giving personal information
Paragraph 1: Basic personal information
Paragraph 2: Information about my family
Paragraph 3: Hobbies
Paragraph 4: Favourite subject(s) at school
Paragraph 5: Asking for a reply

A
In my free time, I like doing sport with my friends. We play all types of sport – football, basketball, tennis. We aren't very good, but we enjoy ourselves ☺.
I also enjoy reading and watching TV.

B
I live with my mum and my little brother. His name is Tom and he's only nine years old. My mum is an artist. She does illustrations for books and magazines. She's very good and she loves her job! My parents are divorced and I don't see my father very often.

C
Anyway, it's time to do my homework. Write back soon and tell me about yourself.
Best wishes

D
Hi!
I'm Steve. I'm 15 and I'm from Portsmouth in England. Let me tell you about myself.

E
At school my favourite subject is English. At the moment we're studying American literature and I'm really enjoying it. I also like studying art. My mum helps me with that, of course!

1 D
2 ____
3 ____
4 ____
5 ____
Steve

2 Complete the information with the correct items.

> Anyway • Best wishes • ☺ • Hi • I'm

1 We often finish emails with this phrase. ____
2 We can use this to show how we're feeling. ____
3 We use this to change the subject. ____
4 We use contractions like this in an informal email.
____
5 We usually start informal emails with this word.
____

3 Look at this personal information. Imagine that you are this person. Write an informal email using the paragraph plan and the email in 1 as a model.

Paragraph plan
Paragraph 1: Mariela, 14, Buenos Aires, Argentina
Paragraph 2: Mother and father, two sisters. One sister 21, other 19. Both at university. Go out with them at weekend.
Paragraph 3: Main hobby – cinema (Italian films). Go often. Also like books.
Paragraph 4: Favourite subject – geography. Good teacher. Also history.
Paragraph 5: Ask for a reply

STUDY SKILLS
When you finish writing, what do you need to check?
➤ STUDY SKILLS page 94

Revision: Unit 1·2·3·4·5·6·7·8·9·10

Grammar

1 Complete the sentences with the present simple form of the verbs given.

1 Elizabeth .... (watch) the news twice a day.
2 My friends .... (not read) magazines.
3 Sunny weather .... (make) me feel happy.
4 A: .... it .... (rain) a lot in your country?
   B: Yes, it ....
5 My brother usually .... (study) in his bedroom.
6 .... you .... (see) friends every weekend?
7 I .... (not think) that's a good idea.
8 How often .... your grandparents .... (visit) you?

2 Complete the dialogue with the present continuous form of these verbs.

> begin • carry • come • not stay • put

Katie: Why (a) .... you .... your books in your bag? The lesson (b) .... now.
Lucy: I (c) .... because I have a doctor's appointment.
Katie: Where's the teacher anyway?
Lucy: He (d) .... now. He's walking slowly because he (e) .... the laptop and some dictionaries.

3 Complete the text with *a/an*, *the* or 0.

I've got (a) .... sister called Polly. My sister loves (b) .... Italian food. She's got (c) .... Italian friend who has (d) .... restaurant. (e) .... restaurant is near our house. We went to (f) .... restaurant last week. We had (g) .... lovely waiter. I'd like to be (h) .... waiter. It's (i) .... good job. I think (j) .... tips are good at their restaurant, too!

Vocabulary

1 Who are these people in a family?

1 the brother of your father ....
2 the brother of your husband or wife ....
3 your father's new wife ....
4 your sister's daughter ....
5 the man a woman is married to ....
6 the father of your father ....
7 the daughter of your aunt ....
8 a person with no brothers or sisters ....

2 Complete the words to find different life stages.

1 ....i...t....
2 ....d....l........e....c....
3 ....e.......h
4 ....h........d....o........
5 ....l........g....

3 Match the words (1–4) to the definitions (a–d).

1 divorced ....
2 senior citizen ....
3 middle-aged man/woman ....
4 single ....

a a person over the age of 65
b a person who was married, but isn't now
c a person who is about 50
d a person who isn't in a relationship

4 Use the suffixes to make nouns.

> -ence • -ment • -ion

1 discuss ....
2 different ....
3 improve ....
4 argue ....
5 inform ....
6 describe ....
7 concentrate ....
8 confident ....

2 Who did it?

Vocabulary

1a Find eight crimes in the word search.

S	H	O	P	L	I	F	T	I	N	G	G	P	X	H	O	U
I	R	Y	F	C	S	X	Z	Y	R	U	Z	I	E	L	K	B
H	O	T	K	R	H	Z	M	Z	T	V	Y	R	C	V	Q	U
I	B	B	Y	V	A	Y	C	G	T	A	F	A	J	A	X	R
G	B	W	W	D	C	U	N	G	H	N	G	C	T	W	S	G
I	E	O	O	R	I	I	D	P	E	D	U	Y	M	N	N	L
V	R	Z	J	R	G	G	Q	R	F	A	C	P	Q	I	E	A
C	Y	N	I	I	G	L	O	P	T	L	S	I	G	A	L	R
F	W	P	A	U	J	M	A	H	K	I	T	G	S	L	H	Y
K	F	E	M	Y	P	X	J	R	V	S	U	R	K	E	O	D
V	D	R	T	L	H	C	I	Z	Y	M	B	A	W	N	N	V

1b Write the words from 1a in column A. Put them in alphabetical order.

	A: crimes	B: criminals
1	burglary	
2		
3		
4		
5		
6		
7		
8		

2 Complete column B with the correct words.

STUDY SKILLS

Why is it good to guess information about words before you look them up in a dictionary?
➤ STUDY SKILLS page 94

3 Complete the sentences with the correct form of the words from 1 and 2.

1 The .... stole money from our home.
2 The police arrested a group of .... who were breaking shop windows last night.
3 A .... attacked an old woman last night and took her handbag and watch.
4 Small shops lose thousands of pounds a year because of ....
5 .... make thousands of illegal copies of DVDs.
6 The .... stole televisions from the shop.
7 Criminals made thousands of dollars last month in seven bank ....

4 Complete the sentences with these words.

> accusing • analysing • arrested • charge
> investigating • prove • questioned

1 The police are .... a case of robbery.
2 They collected evidence and now they are .... it.
3 This morning they .... a suspect and .... him for an hour.
4 However, they didn't .... him because they can't .... that he was the robber.
5 The newspapers are .... the police of being slow.

5 Complete the sentences with the noun form of the words given.

1 The police are still looking for .... that their .... committed the crime. (prove, suspect)
2 After .... of new evidence, the police reopened the .... (analyse, investigate)
3 Police have got a man at the station on a robbery ...., but he is denying the .... (charge, accuse)
4 Police found a .... of watches in the criminal's car when they made the .... (collect, arrest)

VOCABULARY EXTENSION

6 Put the letters in order to find a verb for each crime in 1.

1 blegru — burgle
2 gum — ....
3 mmciot rfadu — ....
4 tripea — ....
5 bor — ....
6 fitposhl — ....
7 least — ....
8 lavanised — ....

Unit 2 I can talk about crimes, criminals and detective work

Reading

1 Look at the photos of two detectives. When do you think they first appeared in books? Read the text quickly and check your answers.

- a in the 1920s
- b in the 1940s
- c in the 1960s
- d in the 1970s

STUDY SKILLS

Why is it useful to look at pictures and the title of texts before you read them?

➤ STUDY SKILLS page 94

Detectives with a difference

Today's article looks at two famous, but quite different, fictional detectives. Who is your favourite?

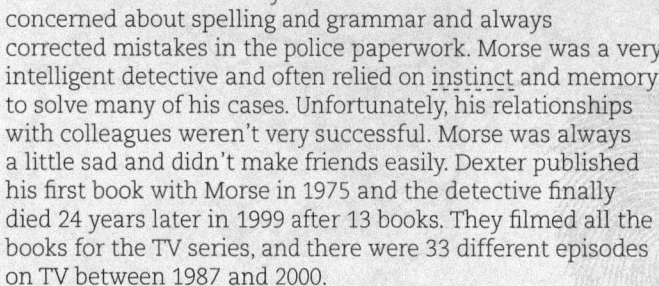

Perhaps the most famous writer of crime fiction in the world was Agatha Christie. Her little Belgian detective, **Hercule Poirot**, is quite an unforgettable character. Poirot first appeared in 1920 in the book *The Mysterious Affair at Styles*, and then continued to solve crimes in 33 novels, one play and 50 short stories before he died in the book *Curtain* in 1975. Poirot is memorable for his appearance and he was very vain. He wore smart, fashionable clothes that didn't always look good on his shape and height – he was only one metre 62 centimetres tall and quite overweight. People often compare Poirot with Sherlock Holmes, but their methods of solving crime weren't the same. Holmes was always analysing tiny pieces of evidence. Poirot preferred to look at the psychology of people to find out why people committed crimes. Although *Curtain*, Christie's final novel about Poirot, was published in 1975, Christie actually wrote the book almost 40 years earlier. She kept the book in a bank, but didn't publish it until just before her own death in 1976. Today, Poirot is well known to millions of people worldwide because of the TV adaptations of the stories.

Another famous detective is **Inspector Morse**. However, most people know Morse because of the television programme and not the original books by Colin Dexter. Morse was a well-educated man but he failed at university. He was concerned about spelling and grammar and always corrected mistakes in the police paperwork. Morse was a very intelligent detective and often relied on instinct and memory to solve many of his cases. Unfortunately, his relationships with colleagues weren't very successful. Morse was always a little sad and didn't make friends easily. Dexter published his first book with Morse in 1975 and the detective finally died 24 years later in 1999 after 13 books. They filmed all the books for the TV series, and there were 33 different episodes on TV between 1987 and 2000.

2 Read the article again. Choose the best answers.

1 What is important about *The Mysterious Affair at Styles*?
  - a It was Agatha Christie's first novel.
  - b The book was extremely successful at the time.
  - c It is the book where we first meet Poirot.

2 What was wrong with Poirot's clothes?
  - a They weren't fashionable.
  - b He chose the wrong clothes for his size.
  - c He didn't wear the right clothes for a detective.

3 When did Christie publish her final Poirot book?
  - a 1945
  - b 1975
  - c 1976

4 What did Inspector Morse never do?
  - a finish university
  - b remember information about his investigations
  - c speak to his colleagues

5 How did most people find out about Morse?
  - a They read the books.
  - b They watched the TV series.
  - c They heard about him from friends.

6 Why did Morse correct paperwork?
  - a He liked to be tidy.
  - b He liked words to be correct.
  - c He didn't like the other detectives.

3 **CRITICAL THINKING**

Read the opinions about detective fiction. Which say that crime fiction isn't a good thing?

1 It helps people understand criminal behaviour.
2 It makes us accept crime as a normal thing.
3 Some people copy things they read in books or see on television.
4 It's important to read about crime and maybe we can prevent crimes happening.
5 It makes you think the world is dangerous.
6 Reading it makes people use their brains more.

4 Match the underlined words with the definitions.

1 the first example of something ....
2 easy to remember because of being special ....
3 very worried about your own appearance ....
4 a natural feeling or ability in a situation ....
5 a particular way of doing something ....

Grammar in context

1 Complete the grammar rules with these words.

> appeared • did • didn't • was • weren't

1 Regular past simple affirmative verb:
   Poirot first .... in 1920.
2 Past simple negative verb:
   She .... publish it until 1976.
3 Past simple question:
   .... you watch Morse on TV last night?
4 *be* in past simple affirmative:
   Morse .... concerned about spelling.
5 *be* in past simple negative:
   Their methods .... the same.

2 Write the past simple form of the irregular verbs in the correct column.

> break • bring • buy • catch • cut • draw • drink
> put • sell • shut • sing • sink • speak • take
> teach • tell • think • throw

-aught	-ang	-ank

-ew	-oke	-old

-ook	-ought	-ut
	bought	

3 Complete with the past simple form of the verbs.

> become • catch • go • not have • steal

Ronnie Biggs **(a)** .... famous in 1963 for his part in the Great Train Robbery. A gang of criminals **(b)** .... 2.6 million pounds from a train. Biggs **(c)** .... a big part in the crime, but the police **(d)** .... him and he **(e)** .... to prison.

> change • escape • leave • recognise • work

Two years later he **(f)** .... to Paris and **(g)** .... his appearance. In 1970 he **(h)** .... France. Then, in Australia, he **(i)** .... in a TV studio, but a reporter **(j)** .... him.

> allow • become • come • die • fly • live

Because of this, Biggs **(k)** .... to Brazil where he **(l)** .... with his family for many years. He **(m)** .... back to prison in England in 2001. He **(n)** .... very ill in 2009 and they **(o)** .... him to leave prison. He **(p)** .... in 2013.

4 Write questions about Ronnie Biggs using the prompts below.

1 When/be born?
   When was he born?
2 What crime/commit?
   ....
3 How much/steal?
   ....
4 police/catch him?
   ....
5 Why/fly to Brazil?
   ....

5 These statements are incorrect. Correct them using the example as a model.

1 Ronnie Biggs was born in 1919.
   Ronnie Biggs wasn't born in 1919. He was born in 1929.
2 Ronnie Biggs committed fraud.
   ....
3 Biggs stole 2.6 million dollars.
   ....
4 He ran away to Madrid.
   ....
5 A police officer recognised him in Australia.
   ....

GRAMMAR CHALLENGE

6 Read the text. Find and correct 12 mistakes.

When I was very young some of my friends taked me to a shop to get the sweets. They hadn't any money so one of them putted some sweets in his pockets, but he didn't paid for them. I liked chocolate bars (and I am still liking them now) so I put an bar in my pocket. But the assistant seed me. He callt the manager of the shop and he phoned my parents. I did feel terrible. I were only five years old, but I am remember it now and feel very embarrassed.

Developing vocabulary and listening

1 Complete the phrasal verbs with these words.

> come • find • look • look • turn • work

1. .... out = discover
2. .... into = investigate
3. .... for = try to find
4. .... up = arrive or appear unexpectedly
5. .... across = find by accident
6. .... out = solve a problem by considering the facts

2 Circle the correct alternative.

1. When I lost a contact lens, I *looked for/looked into* it everywhere.
2. The maths problem was really difficult, but after thinking hard, they *worked out/came across* the answer.
3. We called the police, but they didn't *turn up/come across* until 9 pm.
4. I lost my bag last week and someone *came across/looked into* it in the park. Unfortunately, it was empty.
5. When she *looked into/found out* that he was lying, it was a terrible shock.
6. They can't make a decision about this question yet. They need to *look for/look into* the facts.

3 LISTENING ▶ 05 Listen to a girl talking about a detective series and answer the question.

Which city is the Rebus series set in?

....

4 ▶ 05 Listen again. Are the statements True (T), False (F) or is the information Not Mentioned (NM)?

1. The name of the inspector in the books is Ian Rankin. — T / F / NM
2. We learn some things that visitors to Edinburgh don't know. — T / F / NM
3. Rebus is popular with his colleagues. — T / F / NM
4. The inspector is a neat and tidy man. — T / F / NM
5. Ger Rafferty is a policeman. — T / F / NM
6. The inspector is a young man. — T / F / NM
7. Rebus committed some crimes himself in the past. — T / F / NM
8. The author is writing more books about the inspector. — T / F / NM

5 Complete these sentences from the listening with phrasal verbs from 1.

1. I enjoy .... puzzles.
2. When you read them you .... a lot about the city.
3. Rebus .... all sorts of crimes.
4. He .... some interesting people while he's .... thieves and robbers.
5. Rafferty .... in lots of the books.

VOCABULARY EXTENSION

6 Use your dictionary to match these phrasal verbs with *look* with their meanings.

1. look after ....
2. look ahead ....
3. look back ....
4. look forward to ....
5. look out for ....
6. look round ....

a. plan what you are going to do in the future
b. feel happy or excited that something is going to happen
c. walk around a room, building or place and see what is there
d. look carefully at people or things around you to find a particular person or thing
e. think about a time or event in the past
f. take care of someone or something

7 Complete the sentences with these prepositions.

> after • ahead • back • forward • out • round

1. Let's look .... this museum slowly. I think it will be interesting.
2. I'm looking .... to the football match tomorrow. I'm really excited about it.
3. We need to look .... and see what problems there could be in the next few years.
4. Mum and I are going out now. Look .... your little sister until we get back.
5. Stop spending your time looking .... Live your life now and enjoy every moment!
6. When you go to the party, look .... for Helen and Kate because they said they were going, too.

I can use phrasal verbs to talk about investigating and finding   Unit 2   15

Grammar in context

1 Circle the correct alternative to complete the rule.

We make the past continuous by using the *present/past* of the verb *be* + *present/past* participle.

2 Match the sentences (1–5) with the uses (a–e).

1 I found out a lot about the city while I was reading the series.
2 Rebus met Rafferty in one of the first books and they became friends.
3 It was raining heavily in Edinburgh.
4 While I was walking round, I was thinking about all the places in the books.
5 Rebus retired because he was too old.

a an activity in progress in the past
b a completed action in the past
c two completed actions in the past
d an activity in progress in the past interrupted by another action
e two activities in the past that were in progress at the same time

3 Complete the dialogue with the past continuous form of the verbs in the box.

do • do • feel • have • not feel • sit • talk • visit

Helen: I rang you at 8 pm last night, but there was no answer. What (a) .... you ....?

Luke: My mum and I (b) .... my grandmother in hospital.

Helen: Why was she in hospital?

Luke: Yesterday morning she (c) .... well, so we called the doctor and he said that she needed to go to hospital.

Helen: What (d) .... she .... last night when you visited her?

Luke: She (e) .... on a chair, not lying in bed. All the patients (f) .... dinner and they (g) .... and laughing. She looked OK. When my mum phoned the hospital this morning, she (h) .... much better.

Helen: That's good news.

4 Complete the text with the past simple or past continuous form of the verbs given.

One Saturday afternoon, a team of police officers (a) .... (play) football against a group of local people in Yorkshire, England. The police officers (b) .... (lose) 2–0 when suddenly an officer (c) .... (recognise) one of the men who (d) .... (play) in the other team. He (e) .... (know) that the man was a criminal. The police officers (f) .... (look) for him for several burglaries. The police officers (g) .... (stop) playing and (h) .... (arrest) the man. Then they (i) .... (start) the match again. In the end, the police officers (j) .... (win) the match 3–2! And the man (k) .... (go) to prison for a long time.

5 Write questions for these answers.

1 *What were you doing at 7 pm last night?*
I was listening to my MP3 player at 7 pm last night.

2 ....
My family was watching a film at 7 pm.

3 ....
After the film I took the dog out for a walk.

4 ....
No, I wasn't sleeping at 9 pm.

5 ....
At 11 pm I was reading.

6 ....
I went to sleep at about 12 pm.

GRAMMAR CHALLENGE

6 Cross out the ten extra words in the text.

Last night we were watching a film on TV when suddenly we did heard a sound. At first we thought that it was came from the TV, but then we realised the noise came from the kitchen.
My dad he thought it was a burglar and so went to the kitchen to be see if he was right. He was opening the door when that something flew out really fast! Then there did was another sound. We went back to the living room. The lamp was on the floor. In the corner there was a parrot. My family and I we recognised it – it was my neighbour's parrot. The parrot was knocking things onto the floor while it is was flying through our house. We did rang the neighbour and he came to take his parrot back. So we didn't see of what happened in the film we were watching.

Developing speaking

1 Complete the expressions with the correct words.

1 Oh ....!
2 I'm .... sorry.
3 It doesn't ....
4 Don't .... about it.
5 I .... terrible.
6 Never ....
7 That's the .... time I ....
8 I'm really, ... sorry.
9 It's not .... important.
10 .... me talk to her now.
11 I'll .... it up to you.
12 It's .... a T-shirt!

2 LISTENING ▶ 06 Listen to the dialogue and check your answers. Which four expressions do you not hear?

3 Put the expressions from 1 in the correct boxes.

Making apologies	Responding to apologies
1	

4 Put the dialogue in the correct order.

a ☐ Jo: I'll make it up to you. You can borrow my new black top if you like.
b ☐ Mia: You know the T-shirt I lent you yesterday? Could I have it back? I want to wear it to the cinema.
c ☐ Mia: Thanks. But it doesn't matter. I'll wear something else.
d ☐ Jo: Oh no! You can't have it now! It's dirty.
e ☐ Jo: I'm really, really sorry, but I got orange juice on it yesterday. I wanted to buy you a new one, but I didn't have time.
f ☐ Mia: Why? What happened?
g ☐ Mia: Never mind. It's just a T-shirt. I've got lots more!

💬 PRONUNCIATION

5 ▶ 07 Which words are stressed in the sentences? Listen and check.

1 I felt awful.
2 I'm so sorry.
3 That's the last time I lend you anything.
4 Don't worry about it.
5 Oh no!

🔍 DESCRIBING PICTURES

6 Look at the photo and write your answers to the questions in your notebook. If you're not sure of something, use *I think* and/or *I imagine*.

1 Who can you see in the photo?
2 Where are they?
3 What are they doing?
4 What do you think of this crime? Why?

7 LISTENING ▶ 08 Listen to a student talking about the photo. Complete the text.

I think this is in a **(a)** .... – maybe a supermarket, but not a very **(b)** .... one. It might be one of those small shops that you **(c)** .... on the corner of the street. I **(d)** .... see a man inside the shop. He's **(e)** ...., maybe around 50, and he's wearing a **(f)** .... suit and tie. He's putting something into his **(g)** .... jacket pocket. I think it's a **(h)** .... and I imagine he's **(i)** .... it. I think this crime happens a lot these days. It's very **(j)** .... because sometimes the owners of small shops **(k)** .... earn much money.

8 SPEAKING Now look at the second photo and answer the same questions.

Developing writing

1 Read the blog post by a girl called Sonya. What crime is the blog about?

a stealing boots from a shop
b stealing a woman's handbag
c a street fight between two men

Sonya's BLOG

What an amazing day last Saturday! Did you see it in the news? I was shopping with my friend Will and we were walking along the High Street. We were looking in the shop windows because I wanted to buy some new boots for the winter. The street was full of people.

(a) .... we heard a loud noise. An old woman was shouting. **(b)** .... I had no idea what was happening. **(c)** .... we saw the woman on the pavement. She was fighting with a younger woman. The younger woman was trying to take her handbag! **(d)** .... everyone was standing looking at them. No one was helping! **(e)** ...., the woman got the bag and started to run away. She was coming straight towards us. Other people moved aside because they were scared. But I was really angry. I put my foot out and she fell over it. **(f)** .... Will sat on top of her and I called the police.

(g) .... the police came and took her away in a car. We gave the woman her bag back and she was very happy. **(h)** ...., the story was in the newspaper with a picture of me!

2 Complete the blog post with these words.

> at first • but • in the end • next •
> suddenly • the next day • then • then

3 Imagine that you were waiting for a friend outside a book shop last Saturday and that you saw the scene on the left inside. Write your blog post. Think about these questions.

1 What were you doing?
2 Who were you with?
3 Why were you there?
4 What happened?
5 What did you do?
6 What happened in the end?

Unit 2 I can write a blog post

Revision: Units 1·2 3·4·5·6·7·8·9·10

Grammar

1 Complete the sentences with the present simple or past simple form of the verbs given.

1 I .... (watch) a detective programme and then I went to bed.
2 Jack's bike .... (not be) outside his house this afternoon.
3 I .... (not enjoy) the concert last week.
4 .... (you/like) stories about detectives?
5 Where .... (you/be) last night?
6 Martha .... (go) to Turkey for a holiday twice a year.

2 Complete the sentences with the present continuous or past continuous form of the verbs.

> cook • do • study • tell • walk • watch

1 At 3 pm I .... at school.
2 When we saw Rita, my friend and I .... through the park.
3 My sister .... me about her day at school when Mum came home.
4 Something smells good. .... your mum .... dinner?
5 When Sally arrived we .... a documentary on television.
6 Please be quiet, I .... my homework.

3 Complete the text with the past simple or the past continuous form of the verbs given.

One day, when I (a) .... (walk) to school, I (b) .... (see) something unusual. A woman (c) .... (sing) and a lot of people (d) .... (watch) her. I (e) .... (not recognise) her, so I continued on my way to school, but when I (f) .... (arrive), nobody (g) .... (be) there. Half an hour later, all the other students (h) .... (come). They (i) .... (talk) about a surprise concert by our music teacher in the street!

Vocabulary

1 Complete the sentences with the correct words.

1 The police arrested a s................... .
2 V................... threw paint all over the director's car.
3 The police are collecting e................... for the case.
4 The punishment for t................... of large amounts of money is usually prison.
5 My sister s................... my clothes, but that's not really a crime.
6 Police suspect those men robbed the bank, but they can't p................... anything.

2 Write words for the definitions. They are all crimes or criminals.

1 somebody who steals from houses ....
2 the crime when you trick somebody to get money or something from them ....
3 somebody who attacks another person to steal from them ....
4 the crime of breaking public things ....
5 the crime of copying software, films, etc. ....
6 the person who steals from a bank ....

3 Complete the text with the correct present simple form of the verbs in the box.

> look • look • turn • work

In this story, there is a mysterious theft. A detective (a) .... into the crime. She asks lots of questions and she (b) .... out that a man called Ron Carter is the criminal. She (c) .... for evidence that Carter did it. She can't find anything, but when she suddenly (d) .... up at Carter's house, Carter admits he is the thief.

4 Write words for the definitions.

1 the period of life when you are a child ....
2 the brother of your husband or wife ....
3 the period of life when you stop working ....
4 a child with no brothers or sisters ....
5 an old adult ....

Gateway to exams: Units 1–2

Reading

1 Read the text. Choose the best answer.

GO TO SCHOOL IT'S THE LAW!

The law in the UK and many other countries says that children under 16 need to go to school. When they don't go to school, it's a crime. It's called 'truancy'. Students miss school for a variety of reasons. Perhaps some are bored or perhaps the work is too hard. Some students stay away because their classmates bully them. However, education is very important and students should not miss school.

It isn't easy to stop truancy. Sometimes schools are so big that it is difficult to know who is playing truant. Advanced technology is helping a lot. Many schools are changing their systems for recording who is present and who is absent. In the past teachers always wrote it down, but now it's becoming more common to use computers. In a group of private schools in Tokyo, students put out their hands for examination every morning. A special computer looks at each student's fingers to check their fingerprints. Prison officers use the same technique with criminals in prison. It means that teachers know exactly who is in class and who isn't.

Schools also use technology to tell parents. A school in Scotland uses a system from the US called Phonemaster. It automatically telephones parents when a student is 30 minutes late for school. The phone doesn't stop ringing until someone answers it. In other countries, like Australia, the school automatically sends a text message to parents when their child is not at school.

In some countries, truancy is the parents' responsibility. In the UK, parents pay a fine when their children are often absent from school for no good reason. Last year over 50,000 parents paid fines of more than £60. In the US, Miami police arrested one parent, Mindy Pearl Viera, because her teenage daughters didn't go to school more than 100 times that year.

The police in the Malaysian town of Seremban have a more 'educational' approach. When they find a student who is in the street and not at school, they take them to the police station where there is now a special 'reading room'. The students read books while they are waiting for their parents to come and take them home. Students who don't finish the book take it home and then write a summary of it.

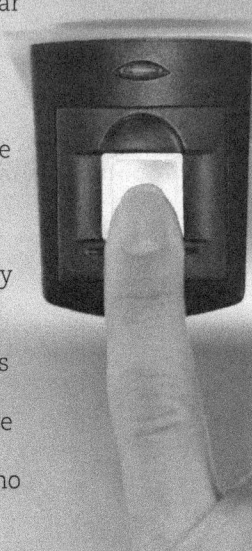

1 Truancy is when …
   a adolescents don't go to school because of illness.
   b teachers send bullies home.
   c children miss school without a good reason.
2 How do many teachers check their students are in class these days?
   a They write their names down.
   b They use computers.
   c They use fingerprinting.
3 When does Phonemaster call a parent?
   a when a student misses a day at school
   b when a student is half an hour late
   c when they don't answer the phone
4 In which country do parents pay money for truancy?
   a The US
   b Australia
   c The UK
5 What do the Seremban police make truants do?
   a go to the reading room in their school
   b read a book from beginning to end
   c write a story

2 Read the text again and answer the questions.
1 Why do some students miss school?
2 Why don't schools stop truancy?
3 How long does the Phonemaster system ring for?
4 How many times did Viera's daughter miss school?

Listening

3 LISTENING 09 Listen to five people talking about being part of a big family. Match the speakers (1–5) with what they say (a–j).

1 Taylor ....   4 Miranda ....
2 Cristina ....   5 Mark ....
3 Ella ....

a thinks their parents expect too much from them.
b has more freedom than their brothers and sisters.
c would enjoy some time on their own.
d has a wider circle of friends because of their family.
e gets annoyed by something a member of their family does.
f comes from a musical family.
g doesn't go into other people's bedroom without an invitation.
h gets a lot of things.
i is not afraid of bullies.
j is an average student.

Use of English

4 Complete the text with the appropriate words.

Last month I (a) _____ to Spain with my mum and dad. It was great. But then, when we came back (b) _____ Saturday morning, we saw that (c) _____ front door of our house was open. We went into the house and all our things (d) _____ lying on the floor in (e) _____ terrible mess. Our TV was (f) _____ there and some of Mum's jewellery was missing. There (g) _____ a beautiful, expensive painting on the wall – but that was gone, too. While we were sunbathing on (h) _____ beach in front of our hotel in Spain, a burglar (i) _____ stealing all our valuable things. We told the police about the burglary but they (j) _____ not seem optimistic about finding the thief. They've had lots of burglaries in this area and they are still looking (k) _____ the burglars. Unfortunately, they don't know who (l) _____ doing them all.

Writing

5 Write an email to a friend. You went on holiday and met an interesting person. Tell your friend about this person. In your email you should:
- say where and when you met this person
- give some basic personal information about them and their family
- give information about their main hobby and favourite subject at school
- say why this person is interesting

COMMON MISTAKES

6 Correct the mistakes in the sentences. In some sentences, there is more than one mistake.

1 My sister's got the new job as the engineer.

2 Are you often going swimming with your friends?

3 Write me soon. Love Paul.

4 When the teacher came into the classroom we were all saying, 'Good morning.'

5 I'm very sorry about that. I'll do it up to you.

6 I was getting home at 4.30. On first I did my homework and the next I phoned Harry.

7 Police caught the burglary last night.

8 My teacher doesn't give us the homework on the Mondays.

9 I work in a clothes shop at the moment.

10 Don't worry about that. It isn't matter.

11 My cousin doesn't like the dogs or the cats.

12 What did you do when I tried to phone you earlier?

3 Universal language

Vocabulary

1 Complete the table.

	Country	Nationality	Language(s)
Mexico City	(a)	(b)	(c)
Warsaw	(d)	(e)	(f)
Tokyo	(g)	(h)	(i)
Bangkok	(j)	(k)	(l)
Brasilia	(m)	(n)	(o)
Cairo	(p)	(q)	(r)

2 Are these sentences True (T) or False (F)? If they are false, correct them.

1 In Russia they speak German.
2 In Switzerland people speak Swiss.
3 People from Bulgaria are Bulgarese.
4 People from Egypt speak Arabian.
5 Argentinian people speak Spanish.
6 In Turkey they speak French.
7 In Brazil they speak Spanish.
8 Austrian people are from Germany.

3 Circle the correct alternative.

1 How often do you *practice/practise* pronunciation?
2 *Translate/Translation* can be difficult sometimes.
3 It's natural to *do/make* mistakes.
4 Last week we *made/took* a listening exam.
5 I enjoy *doing/making* speaking exercises.
6 You need lots of *practice/practise* to write in English.
7 We're going to *revise/revision* for our exam.
8 When learning English, *memorising/making* the new vocabulary helps.

STUDY SKILLS

Why is it useful to reflect on how you learn English?
➤ STUDY SKILLS page 94

4 Complete the sentences with the correct form of these verbs.

x2 do • make • memorise • study • take • write

1 Last week we .... an exam.
2 It's only natural to .... mistakes.
3 Do you enjoy .... speaking exercises?
4 I must .... my homework before I watch TV.
5 Do we have to .... an essay in the test?
6 It's important to .... irregular verbs.
7 Good students usually .... hard for exams.

VOCABULARY EXTENSION

5 Complete the sentences with the prepositions.

down • in • of • off • up

1 I need to hand .... my homework tomorrow.
2 How many words did you need to look .... in your dictionary?
3 I wrote .... everything the teacher said and then I checked it at home.
4 Sometimes I can't think .... any examples.
5 The teacher tells us .... if we speak our own language in class.
6 We often do exercises where we have to fill .... the gaps.
7 It's useful to make .... a story using new words so that you remember them.

Unit 3 I can talk about countries, nationalities and languages

Reading

1 Read the article and choose the best title for it.
  a School children in Finland want more Latin
  b The news in Latin
  c Latin isn't a dead language

What language do people speak in Finland? Finnish? That's true, but some people there also speak Swedish. And there is another language that people speak in Finland which is a little more unusual – it's Latin! In some countries students can learn Latin at school, but it's quite rare for people to speak or listen to this language. They usually write it or translate it. However, in Finland it's a bit different. They can hear it on the radio!

A retired Finnish university professor called Tuomo Pekkanen started the radio programme where his wife, Virpi, reads the news every day on the national radio station … in Latin. The title of the programme is Nuntii Latini and it gives information about five or six short news items before the main news is read in Finnish. Professor Pekkanen started this in 1989 because he believes that understanding Latin is an important part of everyone's education. There are only one or two programmes like this in the world, but the Internet is making them available to lots and lots of people around the world. Thousands and thousands of people listen online and the programme receives a lot of letters from people in about 50 countries.

When he is making his news programme, there are sometimes words which are difficult for Pekkanen to translate because, as you probably know, the Romans didn't have any modern technology like television, computers, emails or lasers. But Pekkanen says that he can talk about many stories on the news by inventing a few new Latin words if necessary.

But Professor Pekkanen doesn't just translate the news into Latin. He also translates the words for songs. And he isn't the only one. Dr Jukka Ammondt, another former university professor, loves Latin, too and he loves the king of rock and roll, Elvis Presley. So what does he do? He sings Elvis in Latin!

There is an important tradition of studying Latin in Finland. There was a Latin congress there recently and people had no problem talking in Latin. Nowadays, English is the language which people all over the world use to communicate. But before English it was Latin. Tuomo Pekkanen believes that around 15 million people in Europe speak or understand Latin today. That's not bad for a 'dead' language.

Dr Ammondt sings Elvis songs in Latin.

2 Read the article again. Are the sentences True (T), False (F) or is the information Not Mentioned (NM) in the text?

1 Some people in Finland speak more than two languages. T/F/NM
2 Students can get quite a lot of practice speaking Latin. T/F/NM
3 Tuomo Pekkanen's main job was presenting the news. T/F/NM
4 The news broadcast in Latin is on television. T/F/NM
5 Pekkanen's wife started reading the news in Latin over 20 years ago. T/F/NM
6 Many countries want to copy Pekkanen's idea. T/F/NM
7 Some words related to modern technology are difficult to translate. T/F/NM
8 Pekkanen sometimes makes up words for the news programmes. T/F/NM
9 Dr Jukka Ammondt worked at the same university as Tuomo Pekkanen. T/F/NM
10 Ammondt is not an Elvis fan, but many Latin speakers are. T/F/NM

3 CRITICAL THINKING

Which of these opinions is expressed in the article?
  a Learning Latin is very important.
  b Technology is helping more people to learn Latin.
  c Modern popular songs are better in English.
  d Young people in Finland aren't interested in Latin.
  e It's possible to make up new words in Latin.

4 Match the words (1–6) with the definitions (a–f).
1 former   4 nowadays
2 items   5 available
3 congress   6 rare

a unusual
b at the present time
c about something someone did in the past
d news stories, pieces of something or objects
e big meeting of experts
f everybody can use it

5 Complete the sentences with the words from 4.
1 Many scientists attended the ....
2 These birds are very .... in the UK.
3 There were five .... in my shopping bag.
4 Everything is more expensive ....
5 Bill Clinton is a .... US president
6 Information is .... for free on the Internet.

I can understand a text about a 'dead' language   Unit 3   23

Grammar in context

1 Complete the table by ticking (✓) the correct boxes. Look at *some* as an example.

	some	any	much	many	a lot (of)	a few	a little
plural countable	✓						
uncountable	✓						
affirmative	✓						
negative & questions							
large quantity							
small quantity							

2 Are these words countable (C) or uncountable (U)?

1 Latin   C / U
2 radio station   C / U
3 language   C / U
4 professor   C / U
5 programme   C / U
6 tradition   C / U
7 information   C / U
8 news   C / U
9 cousin   C / U
10 homework   C / U

3 Circle the correct alternative.

1 Have you got *much/many* close friends?
2 Do you have *much/many* free time?
3 There isn't *much/many* money in my wallet!
4 How *much/many* cousins have you got?
5 Katy didn't give me *much/many* information about the concert.
6 Do you have *much/many* traditions in your country?
7 I don't have *much/many* homework so I can go to the party this weekend.

4 Cross out the alternative that is wrong.

1 I'd like to buy *some/many/a few* magazines please.
2 There isn't *a lot of/any/some* room on this shelf for more books.
3 Can I have *a little/many/some* milk in my tea, please?
4 Do you study *any/many/some* other languages apart from English?
5 There are *a few/a lot of/much* sweets left in the packet.
6 There isn't *much/a lot of/many* money in my wallet!
7 Katy gave me *a little/a few/some* books to read.
8 There isn't *much/a lot of/many* good news in the newspaper today.
9 *A lot/Many/Any* of my friends speak French.

5 Complete the sentences with the words in the box.

> a few • a little • a lot • many • much

1 I don't have .... grapes left – only two.
2 There's only .... milk in the fridge.
3 There are .... of students at my school. It's really big.
4 I don't really have .... free time at the moment.
5 I've got .... ideas for the project, but it's a really difficult topic.

6 Look at the pictures and write sentences with *there is/are* and *a few* or *a little*.

1  There's a little water.

2

3

4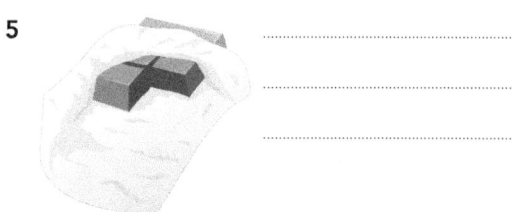

5

6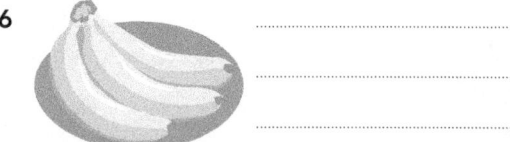

GRAMMAR CHALLENGE

7 Find and correct ten mistakes in the paragraph.

I live in a small village called the Marshwood. There aren't much people in my village. There are only a little houses and shops. However, the shops sell a lots of basic things like the bread and the milk. There isn't many public transport either. There are only a little buses during the week and on Sundays there aren't some. Most of a people travel by car to work in the city.

Developing vocabulary and listening

1 Add the correct prefixes to make negative adjectives.

> un- • im- • in- • ir- • il-

1 ....regular
2 ....happy
3 ....possible
4 ....correct
5 ....visible
6 ....usual
7 ....legal
8 ....formal

2 Use the clues to complete the puzzle and find the word in the shaded column.

1 can't see it
2 not common
3 can't do it
4 not right
5 doesn't follow normal rules
6 sad
7 language used with friends
8 ....

3 LISTENING ▶ 10 Listen to three people talking about people who work with languages. Match the speakers (1–3) with the jobs (a–d). There is one job you do not need.

1 Laura ....
2 Rachel ....
3 Michael ....

a an actor
b a teacher
c a politician
d an interpreter

STUDY SKILLS

Is it necessary to understand every word when you listen to a text in English?
➤ STUDY SKILLS page 94

4 ▶ 10 Listen again and match the speakers with the correct information.

Which speaker …

a found a job using his/her own language? ....
b thinks that a change of environment is good in his/her job? ....
c needs to do his/her job very quickly? ....
d changed his/her ambitions because of a job he/she had? ....
e has to be very accurate in his/her work? ....
f mentions some difficulties about learning a language? ....

VOCABULARY EXTENSION

5 Add the correct prefixes un-, im-, ir- or il- to make these adjectives negative.

1 ....patient
2 ....probable
3 ....relevant
4 ....logical
5 ....responsible
6 ....legible
7 ....official
8 ....practical

6 Complete the sentences with the correct adjectives from 5.

1 What you said is .... – we're talking about something completely different.
2 I can't read your handwriting. It's ....
3 Don't be so .... We'll get there soon!
4 You can't leave a young child on its own – it's ....
5 Your ideas are .... They don't make any sense!
6 It's ...., but you've got the job! You'll hear tomorrow by email.
7 Those new shoes are very .... You can hardly walk in them!
8 Her story was highly .... I didn't believe her at all.

Grammar in context

1 Complete the rules with the relative pronouns in the box.

> that • when • where • which • who • whose

1. We use *that* and .... for people.
2. We use .... and .... for things.
3. We use .... for possessions, about people and things.
4. We use .... for times.
5. We use .... for places.

2 Circle the correct alternative. Sometimes both are correct.

1. I use three languages *that/0* I learnt at school.
2. There are people *who/which* are from many different countries.
3. She's the girl *who/whose* cousin is at our school.
4. I go to meetings *where/that* there are people from many countries.
5. This is the room *that/where* I work.
6. The languages *which/that* I teach are French and Russian.
7. I remember the time *when/which* I first met you.
8. I love Paris. That's *where/0* I first did some acting.
9. He's the writer *who/whose* books are very popular at the moment.
10. This is the bus *which/0* goes to the city centre.

3 Complete the sentences with the correct relative pronoun or *0* if it's possible to leave it out.

1. Russia is a country .... it is very cold in winter.
2. The weekend is a time .... people can usually relax.
3. English is a language .... people speak all over the world.
4. Tennis is a sport .... has many fans in lots of different countries.
5. New York is a city .... they make a lot of films.
6. Chris Hemsworth is the actor .... starred in *Thor*.
7. August is a month .... lots of people go on holiday.
8. That's the man .... wife is famous.

4 Join the two sentences using *who*, *which*, *when* or *where*.

1. 'Greens' is a restaurant. You can get vegetarian food there.
   ....
2. Mr Jones is the teacher. He taught me maths last year.
   ....
3. April is a busy month. We have a lot of tests in April.
   ....
4. *Great Expectations* is a good book. I enjoyed reading it.
   ....
5. Chinese is a complicated language. It's difficult to learn it.
   ....

GRAMMAR CHALLENGE

5 Correct the mistakes in the definitions.

1. The season who is the warmest of the year.
   ....
2. Someone which deliberately damages property.
   ....
3. The period of your life that you change from being a child to being a young adult.
   ....
4. An Asian country where is an island east of South Korea.
   ....
5. An important test of your knowledge, especially one what you take at school.
   ....
6. The woman her your father marries in a second marriage.
   ....

6 Write the word for each definition.

1. Word: s..................
2. Word: v..................
3. Word: a..................
4. Word: J..................
5. Word: e..................
6. Word: s..................

Developing speaking

1 **LISTENING** ▶ 11 **Listen to the dialogue and complete the expressions.**

1 ....? I'm not .... I understood.
2 Does the .... include other activities?
3 Could you .... that?
4 Can you send me a .... form?
5 ....? Did you say on the 30th July?
6 Could you give me some .... about your summer courses?
7 How .... is the course?
8 How long does the course ....?

2 Complete the dialogue with expressions from 1.

A: Good morning. This is the Bradford School of English. How can I help you?
B: Good morning. I'm calling from Italy. **(a)** ....
A: Yes, of course. We have a course which begins on the 13th July.
B: **(b)** ....
A: No, on the 13th.
B: Ah, I understand. **(c)** ....
A: 20 days.
B: Do you organise accommodation?
A: Yes, we do. Students usually live with local families.
B: **(d)** ....
A: You can stay with a family near the school.
B: Okay. Thank you **(e)** ....
A: £950.
B: **(f)** ....
A: Yes, I said the price is £950.
B: **(g)** ....
A: Yes, it does. It includes excursions and social activities.
B: I'm very interested in the course. **(h)** ....
A: Yes, of course. Can you give me your name and address?

3 Which three phrases in the dialogue in 2 do we use to check understanding?

1 ....   2 ....   3 ....

💬 PRONUNCIATION

4 ▶ 12 **Listen and underline the words that sound like one word when we say them, e.g. buy + a = buya**

1 I'm interested in a new course.
2 Sorry, did you say 10th May?
3 Could you say that again?
4 Can I help you?
5 How much is the course?
6 The price is fifty pounds a week.

➕ DESCRIBING PICTURES

5 Look at the photo and write your answers to the questions in your notebook. If you're not sure of something, use *I think* and/or *I imagine*.

1 Who can you see in the photo?
2 Where are they?
3 What are they doing?
4 What do you think they are talking about? Why?

6 **LISTENING** ▶ 13 **Listen to a student talking about the photo. What are her answers to the questions?**

7 **SPEAKING** **Now look at the second photo and answer the same questions.**

Developing writing

1. **Read this language biography by a British student and put the paragraphs in a logical order.**

   Paragraph 1 .... Paragraph 4 ....
   Paragraph 2 .... Paragraph 5 ....
   Paragraph 3 ....

   A I still study French now at secondary school. We read books in French and then we talk and write about them. We also study difficult points of grammar and write down new words that we come across.

   B I started learning French when I was at primary school. I was seven years old. I remember singing songs in French and playing games. We learnt a lot of French words, like colours, animals and clothes.

   C I like to learn French by learning all the new vocabulary at home and then writing it in sentences so that I can remember them. Then, of course, I try to use the new words in class and when I write to my friend.

   D My name is Luke Gallagher and I'm 15 years old. I'm British and my first language is English. Apart from English, I can speak French and German.

   E Apart from doing French at school I also have some contact with French outside the classroom because I have a French e-pal. I send him messages every week and next summer I think I'm going to visit him. He lives in Brittany. I listen to some French singers, too, and occasionally I watch French films at the cinema or online.

2. **Match these titles with paragraphs of the language biography from 1. Write the paragraph letter.**

   1 Language-learning experiences outside school ....
   2 Language-learning experiences at primary school ....
   3 How you prefer to learn a language ....
   4 Basic personal information ....
   5 Language learning experiences at secondary school ....

3. **Which paragraphs would these notes go in? Write the paragraph letter.**

   1 It's good to watch films in class because they're interesting and it's not like learning. ....
   2 My first language is English, but I'm from Wales and I also speak some Welsh. ....
   3 We sang lots of songs and drew pictures and posters of animals with their French names! ....
   4 My best friend and I love French and we often speak it together in the evening and at the weekend. It's hard, but it's good fun and good practice. ....
   5 I'm taking French exams next month and they're quite important. We are doing a lot of grammar, but also we're reading some books and plays in French which is really interesting. ....

4. **Interview a partner about their language learning. Write their language biography.**

Unit 3 I can write a language biography

Revision: Units 1·2·3·4·5·6·7·8·9·10

Grammar

1 Decide if the words in bold are correct in these sentences. If not, correct them.

1 I haven't got **many** money. ....
2 There isn't **some** bread on the table. ....
3 There's **much** orange juice in the fridge. ....
4 Only **a few** people can win a Nobel Prize. ....
5 There were **a little** people at the party. ....
6 I've got **any** pencils that you can use. ....
7 Are there **a lot of** people in the shop? ....

2 Complete the sentences with the correct relative pronoun: *who, that, which, whose, when* **or** *where*.

1 He's the teacher .... helped me to pass the exam.
2 That's the school .... I went when I was five.
3 Do you remember the time .... I fell into the river?
4 She's the girl .... father is an actor.
5 Have you read the essay .... I wrote?
6 This is the email .... came yesterday.

3 Complete the definitions with the correct relative pronoun or 0 if it's possible to leave it out.

1 It's the nationality of a person .... comes from Switzerland.
2 It's the country .... Argentinian people live.
3 It's the man .... father is your grandfather.
4 It's the crime .... thieves commit.
5 It's the person .... copies DVDs and software illegally.
6 It's the period .... you are a child.
7 It's a country .... people speak Portuguese.
8 It's a thing .... you often do after school.

4 Complete the paragraph with one word for each gap.

I went to **(a)** .... shopping centre near my house this morning to buy **(b)** .... clothes, but there were a **(c)** .... of people there so I didn't stay. I went home and looked at a **(d)** .... websites instead. I wanted to find **(e)** .... information about **(f)** .... environment for my school project, but there wasn't **(g)** .... useful information at all.

Vocabulary

1 Write the country or nationality.

Country	Nationality
(a)	Polish
Brazil	(b) ....
(c)	Mexican
(d)	Turkish
Japan	(e) ....
(f)	Thai
Russia	(g) ....
(h)	Austrian

2 Correct the words in bold.

1 Oh no! I **did** a mistake in that exercise. ....
2 Are we **taking** this exercise? ....
3 We need to **revision** before the test. ....
4 I like being a teenager because I can be more **independence**. ....
5 Do you want to **practice** this tomorrow? ....
6 Police arrested the **burglary** yesterday. ....

3 Make the words negative by adding prefixes.

1 ....possible   3 ....legal   5 ....happy
2 ....regular   4 ....correct   6 ....visible

4 Write the nouns from these verbs.

1 revise ....
2 analyse ....
3 translate ....
4 retire ....
5 collect ....
6 discuss ....
7 vandalise ....
8 investigate ....
9 memorise ....
10 improve ....

4 Health watch

Vocabulary

1 Find 12 parts of the body in the word search.

S	H	O	U	L	D	E	R	C	S	D	U
A	C	V	F	A	C	E	U	H	R	L	O
B	J	P	P	U	X	H	E	E	L	D	A
E	I	I	W	T	E	M	T	E	N	M	N
L	H	B	X	R	B	E	Y	K	T	T	K
A	C	F	A	C	W	Z	U	Q	H	H	L
S	T	Z	C	C	H	I	N	I	R	E	
W	H	E	X	K	K	C	K	G	G	O	S
R	U	X	V	K	N	E	E	X	H	A	A
K	M	M	X	J	U	U	Y	F	D	T	K
D	B	B	S	E	G	C	B	Q	K	S	H
Y	U	O	G	Q	L	A	T	P	P	D	H

2 Complete the words about the body with the missing vowels (*a, e, i, o* and *u*).

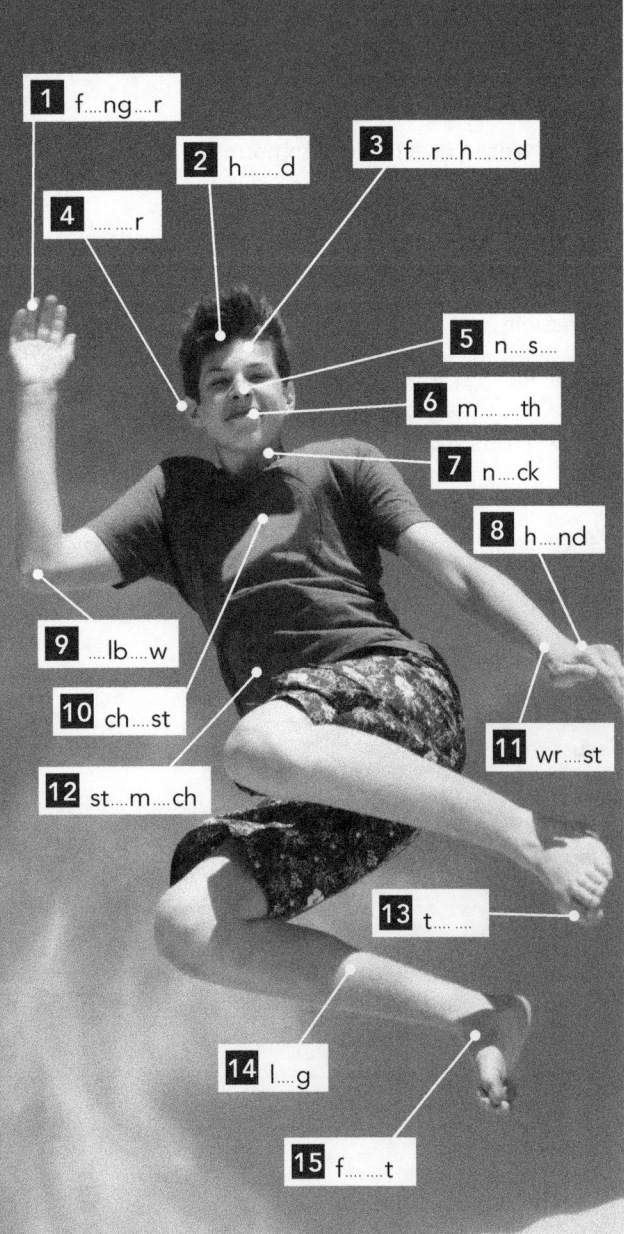

1. f....ng....r
2. h........d
3. f....r....h........d
4. ....r
5. n....s....
6. m........th
7. n....ck
8. h....nd
9. ....lb....w
10. ch....st
11. wr....st
12. st....m....ch
13. t........
14. l....g
15. f........t

3 Look at the pictures and complete the sentences.

1 He's got a .... hand.

2 He's got a ....

3 His finger ....

4 She's got a .... in her leg.

5 She's got a .... leg.

STUDY SKILLS

To learn vocabulary, it is essential to keep a record of new words. Do you do this? How do you organise the words?
➤ STUDY SKILLS page 94

VOCABULARY EXTENSION

4 Complete the sentences with the words in the box.

> bruise • burned • dizzy • rash • sneezing • swollen

1 My ankle is injured. It's very .... and I can't put my boot on.

2 I hit my leg on the table and now I've got a .... on my thigh.

3 I touched a hot plate and I .... my hand.

4 I put too much pepper on my food and now I'm .... all the time.

5 I'm allergic to strawberries! I ate one and now I've got a .... on my arm.

6 I got out of bed too quickly and now I feel ....

Unit 4 I can talk about parts of the body, health problems and illnesses

Reading

1 Look at the picture of someone in hospital. What do you think caused his injury? Read the blog to check.

a an animal   b his bike   c someone else   d an accident at home

TJ's Blog

About me | Contact | Follow

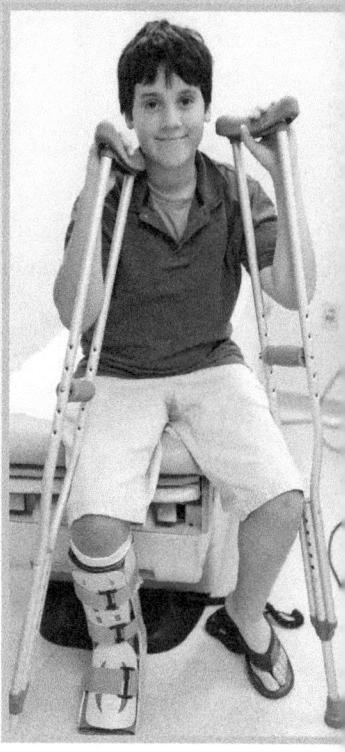

MONDAY
Today's my first day at Brenton Hospital and I'm feeling pretty sad. I've never been in hospital before and it's my birthday today. I planned to go out and have fun with my friends, but I'm here instead ☹. I've been here since they brought me in last night after my accident. I can't believe I did it. I was cycling home when a cat ran across the road in front of me. So I had to <u>brake</u> hard. I was going quite fast down a hill and I fell off the bike and hit the road. I was wearing a <u>helmet</u> so my head was OK, but I couldn't move. A woman was walking her dog when she saw me and called an ambulance. They think I've broken my ankle – and my whole body <u>is killing me</u>! The doctors think that I need an <u>operation</u> – help! I've only been here for a few hours and everyone has been really nice, but I want to go home!

TUESDAY
I've just woken up, but I feel really tired. Two new <u>patients</u> came in during the night, and woke me up and after that I couldn't sleep. Hospitals are noisy places. But there's some good news. The doctor has been to see me this morning and I can go home tomorrow! Luckily, I don't need to have an operation. I just need to rest and use <u>crutches</u> for a while. I've also made some friends here. In the next bed to me there's a boy called Blake. He's broken his wrist. He was in a car accident last night. And opposite me there's Liam. He's hurt his leg and he has to lie down all the time. But he still talks a lot! They're really nice guys, but I still can't wait until tomorrow!

WEDNESDAY
I've arrived home finally! It's so good to be here. My ankle still hurts and they've put a big bandage on it, but I'm happy to be in my own bed again. I have to be careful and sleep a lot. They've also given me some painkillers which really help. But I hope that I can celebrate my birthday with all my friends next week. And soon I think I can go back to school – I have never wanted to go to school so much! ☺

2 Read the posts again and answer the questions.

On which day (Monday, Tuesday or Wednesday) does TJ …

1 talk about a lack of sleep?
2 explain what happened?
3 refer to someone helpful?
4 talk about plans for the future?
5 mention some people he's met?
6 worry about some future treatment?
7 talk about how to get better?
8 mention a missed celebration?
9 talk about something unusual that he has missed?
10 give a short description of the hospital?

3 CRITICAL THINKING

Which statements are fact (F) and which are opinions (O)?
1 TJ has broken his ankle.   F / O
2 He doesn't need an operation.   F / O
3 TJ has learnt a lesson about cycling too fast.   F / O
4 He can't go home yet.   F / O
5 He will write more tomorrow.   F / O
6 The hospital has given TJ some crutches.   F / O

4 Match the <u>underlined</u> words in the blog posts with the definitions.

1 people who are getting medical help
2 to stop or slow down a car or bike
3 hurts a lot
4 sticks that you put under your arms to help you walk
5 a hard hat you use to protect your head
6 when a doctor cuts into a body to repair a problem

5 Complete the sentences with the correct form of the words or phrases from 4.

1 The rash on my arm is so painful. It ....
2 I was on .... for six weeks after my accident.
3 My sister needed an .... when she broke her arm.
4 I hated being a .... in hospital. It was so boring!
5 It's important to wear a .... when you ride a bike.
6 I had to .... quickly when I saw the cat in the street.

I can understand a blog about a health problem   Unit 4

Grammar in context

1 Circle the correct alternative to complete the rules.

  a We make the present perfect with the present simple of *have/be* + the *present/past* participle of the main verb.

  b We use *ever/never* to say at any time in your life and *ever/never* to mean at no time in your life.

2 Complete the sentences with the present perfect form of the verbs given.

  1 I think I ……………… (break) my ankle.
  2 I ……………… (be) here for a few hours.
  3 Sarah ……………… (do) her homework. Here it is.
  4 Alfie and Holly ……………… (live) in Paris for two years.
  5 We ……………… (buy) a dog.
  6 My dad ……………… (paint) this room green. It looks great!
  7 Sam ……………… (have) this watch since he was 12.

3 Match the rules with the sentences from 2. Write a, b or c.

  a an experience or experiences which happened at an unspecified moment in the past
  b a past action which has a result in the present
  c a situation that started in the past and continues to the present

4 Write questions in the present perfect with *ever*. Then write a negative answer with *never*.

  1 Question: you/climb a mountain?
  Have you ever climbed Mount Everest?
  Answer:
  No, I've never climbed Mount Everest.

  2 Question: your parents/visit the North Pole?

  Answer:

  3 Question: you/speak to the Queen of England?

  Answer:

  4 Question: he/win an Oscar?

  Answer:

  5 Question: you/ride an elephant?

  Answer:

  6 Question: your English teacher/star in a film?

  Answer:

  7 Question: you/sing in a concert?

  Answer:

5 Complete the rules with *for* and *since*.

  a We use ……………… with periods of time.
  b We use ……………… with moments in time.

6 Circle the correct alternative.

  1 I have *never/ever* felt so ill.
  2 We have been here *for/since* half past three.
  3 Have you *ever/never* been in hospital?
  4 Liam has been the singer in the band since *three years/2009*.
  5 My sister *has/has had* that bike since she was little.
  6 I've had a bandage on my ankle *for/since* a week.
  7 Have you *ever/never* been to London?
  8 He has *ever/never* met his Australian cousin.

⊕ GRAMMAR CHALLENGE

7 Rewrite the sentences by adding *ever*, *never*, *for* or *since* in the correct place.

  1 Have you been here a long time?

  2 She's wanted to be a doctor she was seven.

  3 Have you met my parents?

  4 I've been to China, but I'd like to go.

  5 Have you worn a suit and tie?

  6 She's been able to walk the operation.

  7 We've known each other ages.

Developing vocabulary and listening

1 Use these words to make one compound noun for each picture.

> aid • attack • centre • first • food • health
> heart • killers • pain • poisoning • room • waiting

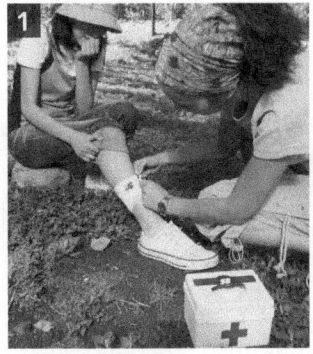

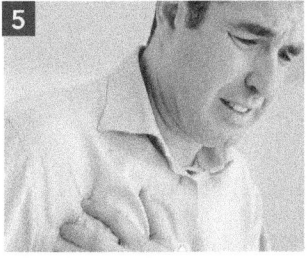
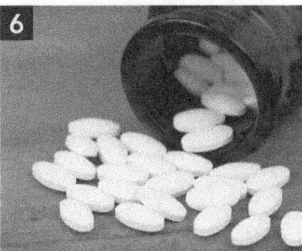

3 LISTENING ▶ 14 Listen to two people talking and choose what they are talking about.

a how many episodes of the series they have watched
b which episode they like best
c what happened in one of the episodes

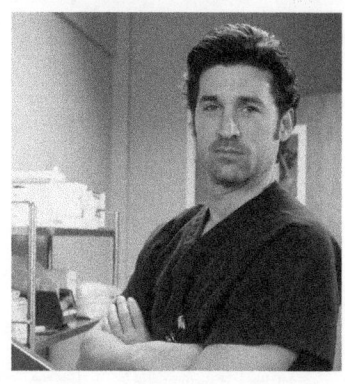

4 ▶ 14 Listen again. Are the sentences True (T) or False (F)?

1 The girl has learnt some first aid. T/F
2 Both speakers have watched the show since it began. T/F
3 Two doctors made a mistake. T/F
4 One of the new doctors has a problem with his head. T/F
5 The doctors find a baby in the waiting room. T/F
6 Jo likes another new doctor. T/F

5 What does the girl think about the information the boy gives her?

a she'd like to know more
b he's given her too much
c she doesn't believe it all

VOCABULARY EXTENSION

6 Match these words to make compound nouns. You can use words more than once. Use your dictionary if necessary.

1 arm .... a bag
2 foot .... b band
3 hair .... c brush
4 hand .... d chair
5 head .... e dresser
6 tooth .... f prints

2 Match the definitions (1–6) with the compound nouns from 1.

1 It's the place where you sit before seeing the doctor.

2 They are the tablets that you take when something hurts.

3 It's a serious medical problem that causes a bad pain in your chest.

4 It's an illness you get if you eat bad food.

5 It's a place where you can go when you're ill.

6 It's the help you give to someone who has been in an accident.

7 Complete the sentences with the compound nouns from 6.

1 He sat down in his favourite ....

2 The detective followed the burglar's ....

3 He cuts people's hair. He's a ....

4 He's got long hair so when he does sport he often wears a ....

5 Some dentists recommend using an electric ....

6 My mum puts everything in her .... – keys, money, mobile phone …

Grammar in context

1 Complete the table by ticking (✓) the boxes.

	just	yet	already
1 We use it for very recent events.	✓		
2 We use it for things that haven't happened, but we think will happen soon.			
3 We use it for something that has happened, possibly before we expected.			
4 We use it in affirmative sentences.			
5 We use it in negative sentences.			
6 We use it in questions.			
7 It usually goes at the end of the sentence.			
8 It usually goes immediately before the past participle.			

2 Write complete sentences saying what the people have *just* done using the prompts below.

1 She/have a shower.
   She has just had a shower.
2 He/win a prize.
3 They/see a horror film.
4 We/do our homework.
5 I/finish this exercise.

3 Complete the sentences with the present perfect form of the verbs given. Put the words in bold in the correct place in the sentences.

1 I (not finish) this exercise. **yet**
   I haven't finished this exercise yet.
2 My sister (arrive) home. **just**
3 Holly and Jack (eat) lunch. **already**
4 My mum (get) back from work. **just**
5 you (see) that film? **yet**

6 you (meet) the new teacher? **just**
7 the bus (go)? **already**
8 We (not study) for the exam. **yet**

4 Complete the sentences with the present perfect or the past simple form of the verbs given.

1 Oliver .... (be) at this school for five years, but he doesn't like it here.
2 I .... (have) this jacket for two years and I always wear it when I go out.
3 That team .... (win) the league in 2005.
4 My friend .... (appear) on TV last summer.
5 .... you ever .... (eat) Indian food?
6 My parents .... (live) in our house for more than 15 years.
7 I .... (buy) a present for you yesterday.
8 We .... (fly) to New Zealand four years ago and we stayed there for a month.

⊕ GRAMMAR CHALLENGE

5 Each sentence contains a mistake. Find the mistake and rewrite the sentence correctly.

1 My friend have lived in this city all of his life.
2 Have you visited Rome ever?
3 His parents have won the lottery in 2006.
4 We have done the shopping yet.
5 I've just seen my cousin ten hours ago.
6 These are my favourite earrings because I had them since I was eight.
7 I have been here since half an hour.
8 I never saw my favourite band in concert.

Unit 4 I can use the present perfect with *just*, *yet* and *already*

Developing speaking

1 LISTENING ▶ 15 Listen to the description of the photo and put the questions in the order that the speaker answers them.

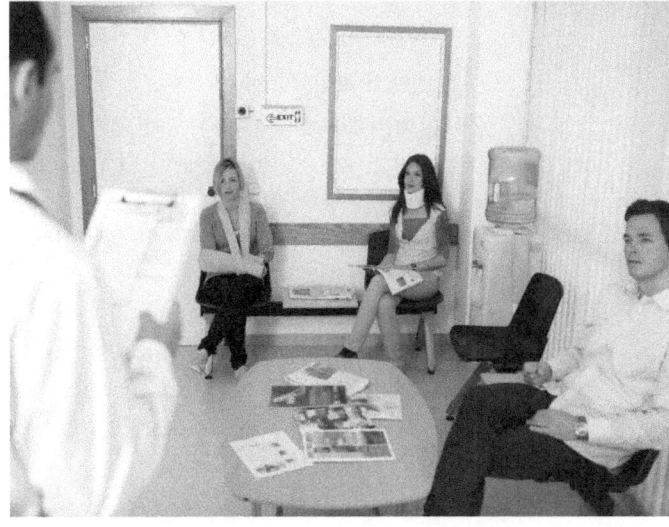

a   What are the people doing? ....
b   When is the scene taking place (morning, night, summer, winter, etc)? ....
c   What do you think about the picture? ....
d   Who is in the picture and where are they? *1*
e   What type of people are they? ....

2 ▶ 15 Listen again and complete the phrases the speaker uses to fill the dialogue.

1   There are four people in the picture and, ..., they're in a waiting room.
2   They look ill, or ...., have health problems.
3   ...., but I think the woman in the middle has got a sore neck.
4   There aren't, ..., any pictures on the wall.
5   .... is, the picture makes me think about times when I've been ill.

PRONUNCIATION

3 ▶ 16 Listen and underline which word is stressed in the compound nouns. Five have the same stress pattern. One is different. Which one?

waiting room   first aid
food poisoning   heart attack
health centre

STUDY SKILLS

What do you do if you don't know the English word for something when you are describing a picture or having a conversation in English?

➤ STUDY SKILLS page 94

DESCRIBING PICTURES

4 Look at the photo and write your answers to the questions in your notebook. If you're not sure of something, use *I think* and/or *I imagine*.

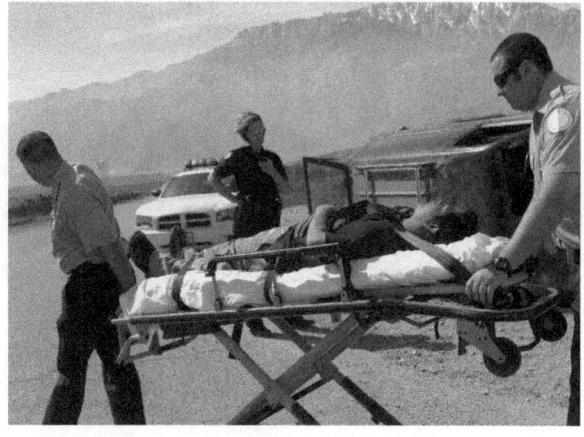

1   Who can you see in the photo?
2   Where are they?
3   What are they doing?
4   How do you think the people are feeling? Why?

5 LISTENING ▶ 17 Listen to a student talking about the photo. Complete the text.

There are four people **(a)** .... the photograph. They are in the countryside near the mountains. One of the people isn't very **(b)** .... I imagine he has fallen over or **(c)** .... he's got a virus. Two people are **(d)** .... him. They are probably going to hospital. In the background there's a car with **(e)** .... lights. I think it's a police car or a small ambulance. I think the man who is **(f)** .... is feeling quite bad. Perhaps his leg **(g)** ....

6 SPEAKING Now look at the second photo and answer the same questions.

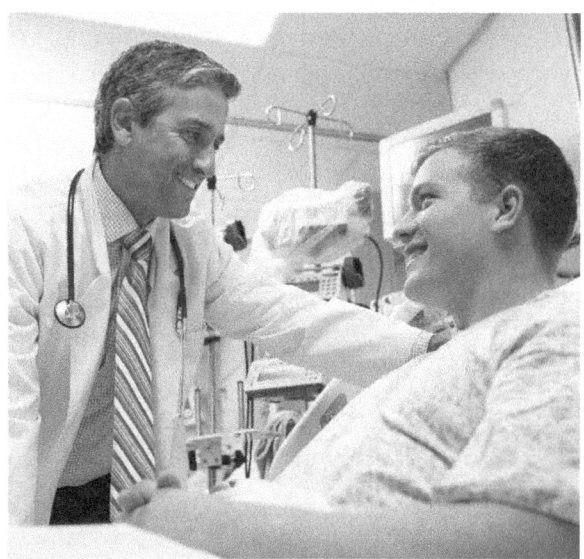

Developing writing

1 Read these instructions. Then look at the note below. Does the writer follow the instructions? Do they write the note in the correct style?

> Your cousin has just passed his driving test. You have gone to his house to see him, but he isn't there. Leave him a note. Include this information:
> - congratulate him on his good news
> - ask him to contact you when he gets home
> - tell him that you have something for him
> - arrange to meet him.

> Marc,
>
> **Congratulations!** Josh has just told me about your test. It's great news! Give me a call **asap**. **I've** bought you a small present and I'd like to give it to you today. When can I see you?
>
> Let me know.
>
> Jenny
>
> **PS** Josh says congratulations, too!

2 Look at the words in bold in the note. Match with the comments about notes and messages.

1 Marc ....
2 Congratulations! ....
3 asap PS ....
4 I've ....

a We often use common expressions like *Great!* when we're writing about good news.
b We often use abbreviations to keep messages short.
c We usually begin with the person's name without *Hi* or *Dear*.
d We use contractions.

3 Write the meanings of these abbreviations.

1 eg ....
2 PS ....
3 ie ....
4 asap ....
5 NB ....
6 etc. ....

4 Rewrite this note to make the style appropriate.

> Dear Joe,
>
> It was wonderful news about your team's win. I'd like to congratulate you!
>
> However I was really sorry to hear about your injured knee. I came round to see you, but your mum said you were still at the hospital. Could you call me as soon as possible when you get home. We all want to celebrate.
>
> Please pay special attention. I left the signed football that you lent me in your bedroom. Make sure your brother has not taken it.
>
> Best wishes,
> Sam

5 Read these instructions and write a note.

> You usually go to a French language class with your friend, Sarah. Today you can't go. Leave Sarah a note. Include this information:
> - tell her why you can't go (an illness? an accident?)
> - ask her to explain to the teacher
> - tell her to call you quickly after the lesson to tell you what homework to do
> - say thank you and arrange to meet somewhere soon

Unit 4 I can write a note

Revision: Units 1·2·3·4·5·6·7·8·9·10

Grammar

1 Write sentences in the present perfect. Put the words in bold in the correct place.

1 you/visit an art gallery? **ever**

2 William/ride a horse. **never**

3 Joe and Ellie/come back from their holiday. **just**

4 I/speak to George. **already**

5 you/write your email? **yet**

6 We/not buy bread. **yet**

2 Complete the sentences with *for* or *since*.

1 Have you been here .... a long time?

2 I've known Magda .... I was 13.

3 Jack's been in hospital .... his accident.

4 I haven't been to school .... a couple of days because of this flu.

5 We've lived in this part of the town .... more than five years now.

3 Complete the sentences with the present perfect or the past simple form of the verbs given.

1 I .... (have) this computer for ten years now.

2 She .... (visit) Argentina in 2013.

3 My uncle .... (live) in Austria since 2012.

4 I .... (be) in the basketball team two years ago.

5 I .... (buy) all of her books. I love the *Hunger Games* trilogy.

6 He .... (forget) to do his homework yesterday.

4 Complete the email with the correct form of the verbs given.

Hi Steph,
I **(1)** .... (write) this from my bed in my bedroom at home! I **(2)** .... (be) home for a couple of hours and it's wonderful. I still **(3)** .... (not feel) well enough to walk round much, but I **(4)** .... (eat) well at the moment and the pain **(5)** .... (disappear) so I feel a bit better. Mum **(6)** .... (bring) me home from the hospital this morning, but she **(7)** .... (go) to work a couple of hours ago. How's the project going? **(8)** .... you .... (finish) it yet? I **(9)** .... (do) some work in hospital, but not a lot. Call me when you've got a minute! I **(10)** .... also .... (email) Karen, so you could both come round after school.
Love
Cathy x

Vocabulary

1 Write the names of the parts of the body.

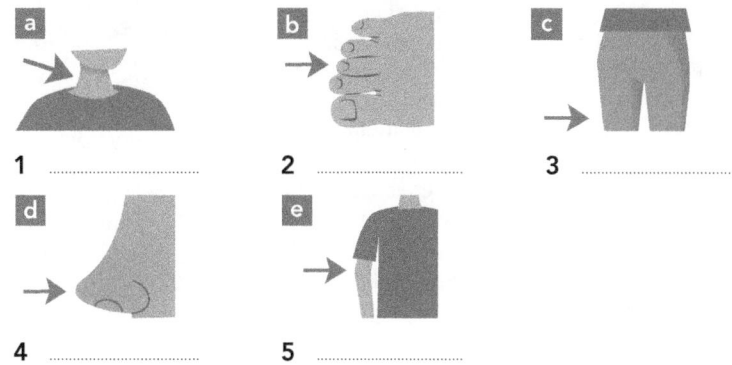

1 .... 2 .... 3 ....

4 .... 5 ....

2 Put the letters of the words in bold in order to find words connected with health.

1 I can't shout because I've got a **rose** throat.
2 Please take a seat in the **ingtawi moor** and the nurse will call you.
3 He had a skiing accident and he's got a **krenbo** arm.
4 When there's an accident, it's good to know **trifs dia**.
5 People who get a bad cold often have a bad **gochu**.
6 Lots of people at school have caught a **survi**.
7 I can't get up because I've got **chackeab**.

3 Match the verbs (1–9) with their objects (a–i).

1 break   a an old diary
2 take   b your speaking
3 work out   c a mistake
4 translate   d an arm
5 investigate   e an answer
6 make   f a crime
7 catch   g a cold
8 practise   h a word
9 come across   i an exam

Gateway to exams: Units 3–4

Reading

1 Read the text about doctors and match each paragraph (A, B or C) with the questions below.

Doctors that changed medicine

A

Hippocrates, an extremely intelligent Ancient Greek, is famous for being 'the father of medicine'. Before him, people knew very little about illnesses. Many thought that magic was responsible for illnesses. Hippocrates didn't believe this. He watched his patients very carefully, asked them questions and analysed their answers. He saw that illnesses come from the things that we eat, the things around us and our habits.

With this observation and information he worked out how to look after the patient. His way of working was completely new for the time. He also told his students that they needed to be serious, professional and, very importantly, to be clean. He made them wash their hands all the time and to make sure the patients were clean, too.

One of the many extraordinary things that Hippocrates did was to discover and use an ingredient called salicin to cure headaches. 2,200 years later, a German scientist rediscovered salicin and it has become an ingredient in today's usual cure for headaches – aspirin!

Medical students remember Hippocrates when they graduate. They make a special promise called the Hippocratic Oath and promise to do everything they can to help people to live.

B

Guy de Chauliac wasn't just a doctor, he was also a surgeon during the 14th century when operations were extremely dangerous. Chauliac became famous when the deadly plague started taking lives in Europe. Many of his friends died and others were afraid and left the cities, but Chauliac stayed and studied the virus. But Chauliac is most famous for writing the 'Magna Chirurgia'. It was a seven volume book which explained surgical procedures. Chauliac finished the book, which he wrote in Latin, in 1363. Later, there were translations of the book into many different languages and the book became an inspiration for surgeons all over the world until the 17th century.

C

Dr Henry Gray was a British doctor. In 1855, he had the idea of producing an anatomy textbook for medical students. He talked about his idea to a young colleague, Henry Vandyke Carter, who was an excellent artist. Gray wrote the text and Carter did the illustrations. They worked together on the book for 18 months, using dead bodies at the hospital for their work. Just three years after its publication, Gray died. He became ill while he was looking after a nephew who had an infectious illness. He was just 34 years old. *Gray's Anatomy* quickly became very popular. This was because the texts were very good, and people especially liked the high quality illustrations. At this time, the medical profession was becoming more serious and students needed to know more to become doctors. *Gray's Anatomy* helped them to do this with all the information it contained. Medical students all over the world still study Henry Gray's *Anatomy of the Human Body*. It has become a classic.

Which doctor …

1 was interested in hygiene?
2 was also a teacher?
3 was able to perform operations?
4 worked as part of a team to produce something?
5 produced a book that is still used today?
6 worked in very dangerous conditions?
7 died because he was helping someone?
8 thought it was important to watch people to find their illness?
9 researched a disease that was killing people?

Listening

2 **LISTENING** ▶ 18 Listen to the talk and complete the sentences with the correct information. Use no more than two words in each gap.

1 The speaker has learned
   (a) .... and
   (b) ....

2 He first learned a foreign language when he was
   (c) ....

3 In his opinion younger children worry less about
   (d) ....

4 His first language teacher's name was
   (e) ....

5 The teacher organised
   (f) .... that were fun to practise new words.

6 He doesn't know much about the
   (g) .... of the language he is studying now.

7 One of his interests is reading
   (h) ....

Use of English

3 Choose the best answer (A, B, C or D) to complete the text.

I'm so sorry to hear you've been ill, Grace. It sounds like a really bad cold. You must stay inside and drink (1) .... of orange and lemon juice for the vitamin C! My sister has had a cold (2) .... Friday, too. It's Wednesday now and she hasn't gone back to school (3) .... She took (4) .... tablets (5) .... my dad bought from the chemist. You should get some too, but don't take too (6) ....! She hasn't got (7) .... left or I could give them to you. How (8) .... water do you drink every day? That's important, too. And stay in a room (9) .... it is warm. Don't worry about school. I only took (10) .... notes in class today, but I'll let you have them. Get well soon!

1	A lots	B much	C lot	D a few
2	A just	B for	C since	D already
3	A yet	B already	C ever	D never
4	A any	B some	C a lot	D a little
5	A whose	B where	C that	D when
6	A many	B few	C little	D lot
7	A some	B much	C any	D none
8	A often	B many	C much	D long
9	A which	B where	C when	D that
10	A few	B little	C some	D a few

Writing

4 Your friend has been away from school because of an illness. He asked you to tell him about any English homework he's missed. Write a note to him. You should:

- ask how he is
- say what you've done in English class
- explain the homework he has to do

COMMON MISTAKES

5 Correct the mistakes in the sentences. In some sentences, there is more than one mistake.

1 I'm afraid I haven't got some free time this week at all.

2 Did you spend many money at the shops today?

3 There's a lots of work to do on this project.

4 The man what wrote the book is on television this evening.

5 Did you already have studied the past simple?

6 I am thinking that the girl in the picture has just win a competition.

7 Could you repeat again that please?

8 London is the city which I grew up.

9 I never have learned Spanish.

10 That sounds like interesting.

11 My cousin has been to Argentina two years ago.

12 Could you to send me some information please?

5 TV addicts

Vocabulary

1 Find eight types of TV programme in the word search. Then write them under the correct pictures. Two types of programme do not have a picture.

Z	Z	H	N	E	Q	I	M	W	Y	R	Q	C
C	F	F	I	L	M	E	O	F	K	S	M	A
H	F	C	X	Z	G	H	W	T	T	M	G	R
A	E	T	Y	D	S	A	R	U	H	S	K	T
T	E	F	F	E	M	E	O	K	E	W	G	O
S	Q	W	M	A	V	V	R	N	N	H	R	O
H	D	A	R	D	L	P	W	E	E	Y	E	N
O	G	D	A	A	N	X	I	O	W	T	A	C
W	J	Q	C	P	L	P	X	O	S	X	H	Y
D	O	C	U	M	E	N	T	A	R	Y	Z	W

1 ....

2 ....

3 ....

4 ....

5 ....

6 ....

2 Complete the TV words with the missing vowels (a, e, i, o, u).

1 ch....nn....ls
2 sw....tch ....ff
3 r....m....t....
4 s....r....s
5 t....rn ....n
6 l....v....

3 Complete the sentences with words from 2.

1 ABC, CBS and Fox are American TV ....
2 *Game of Thrones* and *CSI* are popular TV ....
3 When you don't want to watch the TV, switch it ....
4 When people are bored, they often .... the TV on.
5 I don't want to watch this programme, but I don't want to get up. Pass me the .... control.
6 Some chat shows are .... programmes and you never know what will happen.

4 Put the letters in order to make adjectives describing TV programmes.

| cryas | fromvinetia | ginmov | nuyfn |
| ringbo | rolpupa | wulfa | igixectn |

1 s..............
2 i..............
3 m..............
4 f..............
5 b..............
6 p..............
7 a..............
8 e..............

VOCABULARY EXTENSION

5 Match the words to make new words and phrases about TV.

1 breaking   a episode
2 sports   b readers
3 chat show   c break
4 news   d host
5 advert   e news
6 first   f commentators

6 Complete the sentences with collocations from 1.

1 We watched the .... of the new series and it was amazing.
2 Listen! There's some .... about the missing ship.
3 I admire those .... They're so calm, even if the news is really bad.
4 I often can't understand .... because they speak so quickly.

40 Unit 5 I can talk about television and use adjectives describing TV programmes

Reading

1 **Look at the picture and answer the question. Then read the article to check your answer.**

   What do you think the picture shows?
   a people watching an advert for televisions
   b people watching a talent competition
   c people watching an art exhibition

STUDY SKILLS

Why can it be useful to set yourself a time limit the first time you read a text?

▶ STUDY SKILLS page 95

The way forward

Television is still one of our most popular forms of entertainment. It's cheap and it is both informative and fun. It also brings people together. Many friends and families still watch a show or a soap together, or enjoy live sports programmes together. TV gives people something to talk about at school and at work and it often gets us talking about important issues. However, television – like everything else in the world today – is changing.

The most important influence on television recently has been technology. Computers and the Internet have completely changed the way we get information. They are now changing the way we get our entertainment. Watching films and videos online is becoming more and more popular. PCs, tablet computers and smart phones are now much cheaper than ever before and people are choosing them as their 'first screens.' Today, because life is getting faster and faster, our mobile screens are the best way to watch programmes anywhere we like – in our bedrooms, on trains and buses – even on the beach.

Because of this, TV companies are quickly changing the way they make shows in order to give the viewers what they want. Experts believe that even in our advanced technological world, people still want to watch programmes in real time and feel a part of what they are watching. An important reason for this is social networking sites, like Twitter and Facebook. People love to watch something at the same time as everyone else and then tweet about it or post comments. During a recent Oscars ceremony in the US, over 5 million people posted more than 19 million tweets. And over 37 million people read those tweets! And in the UK a popular game show called Million Pound Drop finds its contestants on social networking sites. The programme makers discovered that more than 12% of the 2.5 million viewers were answering the quiz questions online at the same time as the contestants.

This interaction between viewers and live programmes is definitely going to increase in the future. TV shows have been interactive for quite a long time. Viewers are able to vote by phone or online for contestants in talent shows. Also they can often predict or react to what happens in the show itself. Sometimes viewers can influence the ending of a drama or soap. This will be more frequent in the future. In Israel there is a talent show called Rising Star where there is a video wall between the studio audience and the singers. When viewers vote, their faces appear on the video wall. If the singer gets 70% of the votes, the wall rises.

The next few years will bring a lot of changes to how we get our entertainment. One thing is sure … it's going to be a very interesting journey for the viewers!

2 **Read the article again. Choose the best answers.**

   1 Paragraph 1 tells us that people …
      a prefer to watch sport live rather than on TV.
      b enjoyed TV more in the 1950s.
      c discuss things they see on television.
   2 Television is changing because a lot of viewers …
      a don't like the programmes on TV today.
      b like using their mobile devices.
      c have more than one TV in their homes.
   3 Why is real time TV still popular?
      a It isn't difficult to get it on tablets and smart phones.
      b Viewers like to chat about the shows online.
      c The TV shows are improving.
   4 Million Pound Drop uses the Internet …
      a to see how many people are watching.
      b to find good quiz questions.
      c to find people for the show.
   5 In one new TV show …
      a the studio audience chooses the winner.
      b the viewers change the show as it goes on.
      c people who don't vote can't see the end of the show.

3 **CRITICAL THINKING**

   Are the sentences facts (F) or opinions (O)?

   1 TV programmes today are more interesting than those ten years ago.   F / O
   2 More than 37 million people read tweets about the Oscars ceremony.   F / O
   3 Viewers can change the ending of some dramas.   F / O
   4 Interactive TV programmes will be exciting for viewers in the future.   F / O

4 **Match the underlined words in the article with the meanings.**

   1 a person in a competition
   2 communication/talking to people
   3 a comment on Twitter
   4 happening at the moment
   5 topics/problems
   6 person who watches TV

I can understand an article about TV programmes   Unit 5

Grammar in context

1 Complete the table with the adjectives in the box. Then write the comparative and superlative forms.

boring • easy • fit • good • ~~small~~

Adjective	Rule	Comparative	Superlative
(a) *small*	one-syllable adjectives, add -er or -est	*smaller*	*the smallest*
(b) _____	one-syllable adjectives which end in one vowel + one consonant, double the last consonant and add -er or -est		
(c) _____	two-syllable adjectives ending in -y, omit -y and add -ier or -iest		
(d) _____	adjectives with two syllables or more, use *more* + the adjective or *the most* + the adjective		
(e) _____	irregular adjectives with no set rules		

2 Complete these sentences with the comparative or superlative form of the adjectives given.

1. Smartphones are now _____ (cheap) than before.
2. This year is _____ (hot) than last year.
3. This will be _____ (frequent) in the future.
4. London is _____ (far) from Moscow than Berlin.
5. That was the _____ (bad) day of my life!
6. Television is one of the _____ (popular) forms of entertainment.
7. The _____ (important) influence on television recently has been technology.
8. Tablets are _____ (good) than laptops.

3 Look at this information about Jake, Mark and Ryan. Then complete the sentences with the comparative or superlative form of the adjectives given.

name	tall	talkative	good at sport
Jake	★★★	★	★
Mark	★	★★★	★★
Ryan	★★	★★	★★★

1. Mark *is shorter than* _____ (short) Jake.
2. Jake _____ (tall) Ryan.
3. Jake _____ (tall).
4. Mark _____ (talkative) Ryan.
5. Ryan _____ (good at sport) than Jake.
6. Ryan _____ (good at sport).

4 Rewrite the sentences using comparatives and superlatives. Do not change the meaning.

1. No boy is taller than Jamie in this class.
   Jamie is *the tallest boy in this class*.
2. A bike is lighter than a motorbike.
   A motorbike is _____.
3. Becky is older than everybody in this class except Matthew.
   Matthew is _____.
4. No one in the 20th century was more intelligent than Einstein.
   Einstein was _____.
5. My bedroom is bigger than my brother's bedroom.
   My brother's bedroom is _____.
6. I think a Peugeot 507 is good, but a Ferrari is very good.
   I think a Ferrari is _____.

⊕ GRAMMAR CHALLENGE

5 There is a word missing in each sentence. Write an appropriate word in the correct place.

1. Watching sports live is more exciting watching it on TV.
2. *The X Factor* is popular than any other talent show.
3. Which is scariest film you've seen?
4. The news programme at eight is longer the news at ten.
5. There aren't good programmes on TV tonight.
6. Jasmine is best newsreader on TV.
7. This is the most exciting film I ever seen.
8. I've had a smartphone three months.

Developing vocabulary and listening

1 **Complete the sentences about the pictures. Use the -ed or the -ing form of these adjectives.**

bored • confused • embarrassed • frightened
interested • relaxed • surprised • tired

a She thinks the lesson ....
b She .... of the ghost train.
c He thinks maths ....
d The music ....
e She .... that she wore her slippers to school.
f He .... in the lesson.
g The letter ....
h He .... from the race.

2 **LISTENING** 19 **Listen to the people talk about different events and match the events (1–4) with the speakers (A–D).**

1 an evening watching a documentary
2 a charity event
3 a trip to the cinema
4 a visit to the theatre

Lily
Ben
Sue
Sarah

3 19 **Listen again and choose the best answers.**
1 How did Lily feel?
  a confused   b embarrassed   c disappointed
2 How did Ben feel?
  a surprised   b interested   c tired
3 Sue thought the hotel was …
  a boring.   b relaxing.   c interesting.
4 Sarah thought the film was …
  a disappointing.   b moving.   c boring.

VOCABULARY EXTENSION

4 **Match the -ing adjectives (1–6) with their synonyms or explanations (a–f). Use your dictionary if necessary.**

1 depressing ....
2 disgusting ....
3 exhausting ....
4 worrying ....
5 terrifying ....
6 amazing ....

a very tiring
b horrible, very bad
c very sad
d very good or surprising
e making you unhappy because you think of problems or bad things
f very frightening

5 **Write the -ed form of the adjectives (1–6) from 4. Check your answers in your dictionary if necessary.**

1 .... 4 ....
2 .... 5 ....
3 .... 6 ....

6 **Complete the sentences with -ing or -ed adjectives from 4 and 5.**
1 Yuck! I think eating insects is ....
2 I haven't slept for two nights. I'm ....
3 This programme is very .... It's all about the terrible problems in the world.
4 She hasn't studied. Now she's thinking about her exams and she's very .... about them.
5 I'm really afraid of high places so the idea of going up that mountain is ....
6 John was .... when he passed the exam. He didn't study at all.

Grammar in context

1 Complete the rules with the words in the box.

> as … as • Not as … as x2 • less … than x2
> more … than

1 We use .... to say that two things, people or situations are similar.

2 .... and .... have a similar meaning.

3 .... and .... are the opposite of ....

2 Compare the two things using the adjective and *less … than* and *(not) as … as*.

1 Italy → big → Russia.
  ....

2 Hamsters → dangerous → snakes.
  ....

3 The River Thames → long → the Amazon.
  ....

4 A kilo of gold → heavy → a kilo of rice.
  ....

5 Chocolate → expensive → caviar
  ....

3 Complete the sentences with the correct words.

1 He's 50. He's .... old to be a professional football player.

2 When you're 14, you aren't old .... to drive.

3 I can't buy that computer. It's £600 and I've only got £450. It's too ....

4 She plays the guitar really well. She's .... enough to become a professional musician.

5 Those shoes are size ten and your feet are size eight. They're too .... for you.

4 Rewrite the sentences using *too* or *not … enough*.

1 He's too young to vote.
  He ....

2 I'm not rich enough to buy that.
  I ....

3 Megan isn't tall enough to close the top window.
  Megan ....

4 Her car is too slow to win the race.
  Her car ....

5 That documentary is too boring to watch twice.
  That documentary ....

5 Rewrite the answers using *too* or *not … enough* in the correct place in the sentence.

1 Why don't you go to school now?
  Because it's early. →
  Because it's too early.

2 Why isn't she a professional pianist?
  Because she isn't good. →
  ....

3 Why can't you ride a motorbike?
  Because I'm 14 – I'm not old. →
  ....

4 Why can't you finish reading that book?
  Because it's got 800 pages – it's long. →
  ....

5 Why don't people swim in the Arctic Ocean?
  Because the water isn't warm. →
  ....

6 Why can't you go to New Zealand?
  Because the flight is expensive. →
  ....

STUDY SKILLS

When you do a grammar exercise there are two main things to think about. What are they?
➤ STUDY SKILLS page 95

GRAMMAR CHALLENGE

6 Put the words in order to make sentences.

1 Children not vote old are enough to
  ....

2 Bicycles expensive are motorbikes than less
  ....

3 only seats few There left a are
  ....

4 as tigers Dolphins dangerous are as not
  ....

5 is long Nile the not Thames as The as
  ....

6 a you the of programme about lot got information Have ?
  ....

7 ill stage was actor to The on too go
  ....

8 man yesterday we He's who met the
  ....

Unit 5 I can use *less … than*, *(not) as … as*, *too* and *(not) enough*

Developing speaking

1 LISTENING ▶ 20 Listen to the dialogue and complete the expressions.

1 Why .... we do something?
2 Good ....!
3 Me ....
4 .... we go shopping?
5 I'm not ....
6 I know what you ....
7 How .... taking your dog for a walk?
8 But .... about the weather?
9 I know, ... call Maddy.
10 ....! She might invite us over.

2 Put the words and phrases from 1 into the correct columns.

Make a suggestion	Respond – no/maybe	Respond – yes

3 Put the dialogue in the correct order.

...... B: OK. Where shall we go?
...... A: It's not hurting much now … but I don't want to make it worse. Let's go shopping then!
...... B: I'm not sure – I don't really like Johnny Depp.
...... A: How about going to the cinema? The new Johnny Depp film is on.
...... B: Great. I need to get a present for Dan!
...... B: Good idea, but it's closed on Sundays, remember?
...... A: You're right. Then why don't we go dancing?
...... A: It would be nice to go out tonight.
...... A: OK. How about going to the Salad Social for dinner?
...... B: But what about your ankle – you hurt it last week.

💬 PRONUNCIATION

4 ▶ 21 Put these words into the correct columns. One word has a sound that is different. Which is it? Listen and check.

air • am • ankle • at • game • haven't • made
Maddy • play • rain • sale • shall • taking

/eɪ/	/æ/

➕ DESCRIBING PICTURES

5 Look at the photo and write your answers to the questions in your notebook. If you're not sure of something, use *I think* and/or *I imagine*.

1 Who can you see in the photo?
2 Where are they?
3 What are they doing?
4 How do you think the people are feeling? Why?

6 LISTENING ▶ 22 Listen to a student talking about the photo. Complete the text.

There are four girls in the photo and they're (a) .... at something. They're all teenagers and three of them are (b) .... very close together on the sofa. One girl is holding something in her hand. I imagine it's a (c) .... for a television or maybe for a game? I think it's for a television and they're watching it together. They (d) .... very interested in the programme and I think something exciting is (e) .... on the screen because they are watching very (f) ....! I think they're enjoying the programme and want to see what happens (g) ....

7 SPEAKING Now look at the second photo and answer the same questions.

Developing writing

1 Read the film review and tick (✓) which things (a–j) the writer mentions.

a her opinion ☐
b the actors ☐
c the story of the film ☐
d the prizes it won ☐
e when it was made ☐
f other films the director has made ☐
g the director ☐
h the place it was filmed ☐
i a recommendation ☐
j other films the actors have been in ☐

FILM review ★★★★★

My favourite film from the last few years is *About Time*. It's a British film which was directed by Richard Curtis and stars Bill Nighy and Rachel McAdams. It came out in 2013. I saw it at the cinema, but you can get the DVD or watch it online today.

About Time is a romantic comedy, like Richard Curtis' other famous films – *Notting Hill* and *Love Actually*. It's about a young man who can travel back in time and try to change what happens in his life. His ability to travel through time causes lots of problems and of course he makes lots of mistakes. However, in the end he meets and falls in love with a beautiful girl.

Personally, I love this film because it's clever, and it made me laugh and cry! It teaches us how to be happy with our lives even when things go wrong. I think the music in it is fantastic, too. It also shows us a lot of interesting places in London, including a restaurant where you eat in complete darkness! In my opinion, it's good for a film to be both entertaining and informative.

I would recommend *About Time* to everyone. It's funny, interesting and it makes you think. As far as I'm concerned, it's one of the best films I've ever seen.

2 Complete the expressions in the review.

1 _____, I love this film.
2 I _____ the music in it is fantastic.
3 _____, it's good for a film to be both …
4 I _____ *About Time* to everyone.
5 _____ I'm concerned, it's one of the best …

3 Match the paragraphs (1–4) with the information (a–d).

Paragraph 1 ....
Paragraph 2 ....
Paragraph 3 ....
Paragraph 4 ....

a description of the film
b information about the actors, director and when it came out
c if the writer thinks others should watch it
d the writer's own opinion and reasons

4 Write a review of a film you have seen recently. Use expressions to show your opinion and your reasons. Divide your review carefully using the paragraph plan.

Revision: Units 1·2·3·4·5·6·7·8·9·10

Grammar

1 Complete the sentences with the correct comparative form of the adjectives given.

1 Greece is usually .... than the UK. (hot)
2 I think Sam is .... than Jake. (thin)
3 She was the .... player in the team. (good)
4 That's the .... thing I've ever seen. (silly)
5 Greg is the .... person I know. (intelligent)
6 Do you think rain is .... than snow? (bad)

2 Rewrite the sentences using the words given. Do not change the meaning.

1 Love is more important than money.
   Money .... less
2 I think that biology is easier than maths.
   I think that maths .... as
3 We aren't old enough to see that film.
   We're .... too
4 It's too cold to swim in the sea today.
   It's .... enough
5 Carla's sister is very clever and Carla is very clever.
   Carla is .... as
6 He is too slow to win the race.
   He .... fast

3 Circle the correct alternative.

1 I haven't seen Jim *for/since* three years.
2 Mrs Jones is the teacher *what/who* taught me art.
3 The other students aren't as tall *like/as* Tom.
4 Can you tell me how *much/many* that meal cost?
5 This is *a/the* best book I have ever read.
6 I haven't finished my homework *already/yet*.
7 There weren't *some/any* students at the party.
8 It's *enough/too* hot for me to drink.
9 I've *ever/never* been to the US.
10 I'*m thinking/think* your new television is brilliant.

4 Find and correct a mistake in each sentence.

1 Sorry, I can't talk at the moment because I work.
   ....
2 How long are you live in this road?
   ....
3 There are a lots of good programmes on tonight.
   ....
4 I saw you in the kitchen earlier! What did you do?
   ....
5 The book what I like best is a detective story.
   ....

Vocabulary

1 Complete the types of programme with the missing vowels (a, e, i, o, u).

1 g....m.... sh....w   4 ....dv....rt
2 c....rt....n   5 c....k....ry pr....gr....mm....
3 d....c....m....nt....ry 6 dr....m

2 Match the adjectives in the box with the definitions. There are more adjectives than definitions.

> confused • confusing • funny • interested
> interesting • relaxing • scary • surprised • surprising

1 It's when something makes you laugh. ....
2 It's how you feel when something happens, but you didn't know it was going to happen. ....
3 It's when something makes you want to know more. ....
4 It's when something makes you feel frightened. ....
5 It's how you feel when you don't understand something or a situation. ....
6 It's when something helps you to rest and feel good. ....

3 Find the words.

1 Family members: unisoc   whenep
2 Nationalities: snauris   urktshi
3 Stages of life: dhocdlioh   hadte
4 Crimes: acrypi   grubyarl
5 Parts of the body: butmh   enek
6 Illnesses: ursiv   dolc

4 Complete the sentences with the correct words.

1 Before you see the doctor you have to sit in the w........................ room.
2 At school they teach us how to do first a........................ in case we need to help someone.
3 Four of my answers in the last exercise were i........................ . I only got two right.
4 My uncle isn't old. He's just middle-a........................ .
5 I've got a headache. Have you got any p........................?

6 Planet Earth

Vocabulary

1 Complete the crossword.

Across
1 a long line of very big hills
4 a long turning flow of water
5 an area with a lot of trees, plants and animals
8 an area with a lot of sand, but not many plants and almost no water
9 a piece of land with water all around it

Down
2 an area between two hills
3 similar to 5 across, but here it rains a lot
6 an area next to the sea with sand, where some people go to spend their holidays
7 a big, cold area that covers the land and sea around the North and South Pole

2 Complete the environment words with the missing vowels (a, e, i, o, u). Match them to the correct pictures.

a dr……ght
b fl……d
c gl……b……l w……rm……ng
d gr……nh……s…… ……ff……ct
e ……z……n…… l……y……r
f r……cycl……
g s……v…… w……t……r
h w……st…… w……t……r

1 …………………… 2 ……………………

3 …………………… 4 ……………………

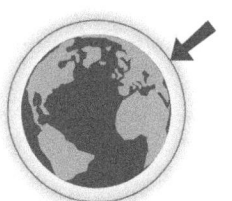 

5 …………………… 6 ……………………

7 …………………… 8 ……………………

VOCABULARY EXTENSION

3 Complete the sentences with these prepositions.

after • away • down • in • up • out • out

1 We throw …………………… too much rubbish these days.
2 Soon we are going to run …………………… of oil for energy.
3 If we cut …………………… too many trees in the rainforest, it can cause problems for the environment.
4 We are building more houses in the countryside and some plants and animals are dying …………………… .
5 The government needs to invest money …………………… renewable energy sources.
6 If we don't look …………………… the environment, we won't have a good life in the future.
7 Companies need to come …………………… with new ways of producing cleaner energy.

Reading

1 Look at the picture and answer the question.

Why do you think the beefburger is important? Read the article to check your answer.

a It's a new recipe.   b It's a new form of cooking.   c It's a new type of meat.

The world's most expensive burger

1 Many chefs today use science to help them create new and exciting recipes. Recently, a top chef cooked a very special beefburger in London and there were pictures and stories in the newspapers about it. But the meal wasn't for a restaurant or cookery book – it was an example of how to solve a growing problem. And the beef in the burger wasn't from a cow – it was from a science laboratory!

2 The world's population is growing fast and by 2060 it will be about 9.5 billion. There is a lot of concern about food. How are we going to provide enough food for everyone? Most people want to have meat in their diet, but if we continue to eat as much meat as we do now, this will definitely be a big problem because it will have an impact on the environment. Firstly, keeping the number of animals that we'll need will increase pollution enormously. It will produce about fifty percent of the amount of pollution that comes from all the planes, cars and other forms of transport. This is because cows produce many different types of gas that are bad for our atmosphere, like methane and ammonia. These cause global warming and acid rain. And secondly, we won't have enough space or water for all the animals – certainly not enough to give them a good quality of life, which is important.

3 Obviously, the easiest answer might be for people to eat less or stop eating meat. Unfortunately, this is probably not going to happen. Most people want to have meat in their diet. Experts say that this is because meat was originally very important in early human development. The calories in cooked meat helped us grow bigger brains! So, the attraction of meat is still part of our nature. This means that we will need to find another way to solve the problem.

4 This is why the beefburger created in London was so important. Scientists today are trying to grow artificial meat in laboratories. They are aiming to produce a food that tastes exactly like beef, lamb or chicken and the beef burger was their first finished product. However – there is still a lot of work to do. The person who ate the burger thought it was quite dry and not very tasty. Also – it cost €250,000. Let's hope the price goes down a lot more before they go on sale at the supermarket!

2 Read the article again and circle the correct alternative. Write the number of the paragraph where you found the answer.

1 The beefburger in London was/wasn't the first of its type.

2 Animals contribute/don't contribute to pollution.

3 Meat was/wasn't very important in the human development.

4 The world's population will keep getting bigger/stay the same.

5 They hope that future meat will/won't have a similar taste to beef and chicken.

6 The beefburger in London attracted/didn't attract a lot of publicity.

3 CRITICAL THINKING

Which of these ideas does the writer agree with? You can choose more than one.

a People will stop eating meat.
b We should limit population growth.
c Animals should have a good quality of life.
d All beefburgers are very tasty.
e We can't continue to produce meat in the same way as we do now.
f Meat needs to be cheap enough for people to afford it.

4 Match the underlined words in the article with the meanings.

1 people's characteristics and behaviour
2 decreases
3 not real
4 very much
5 nice to eat

Grammar in context

1 Complete the sentences with the correct form of *be going to* or *will*.

1. I can't do this exercise! — Don't worry! .... help you!

2. Next week I .... see my favourite group in concert. I've already got my ticket.

3. It .... be my 16th birthday next week.

4. We think that the economy .... get better soon.

5. It looks like it .... be hot today.

2 Complete the rules with *be going to* or *will*. Then match them with the sentences from 1.

a We use .... to make predictions based on some sort of evidence. ....

b We use .... to make a general prediction, often after verbs like *think*, *hope* or *expect*. ....

c We use .... to talk about an objective truth in the future. ....

d We use .... to talk about plans or intentions. ....

e We use .... for decisions that we make at the moment of speaking. ....

3 Circle the correct alternative.

1 A: The phone is ringing.
  B: I*'m going to/'ll* get it.
2 A: Do you want to come to a party on Saturday?
  B: I can't. My family and I *are going to/will* go to London for the weekend.
3 How old *are you going to/will you* be next birthday?
4 He's putting his coat on. He *'s going to/will* go out.
5 It's cold in here. I*'m going to/'ll* close the window.

4 Match the sentences (1–8) with the symbols (a–e).

1 Perhaps it'll rain. ....
2 It definitely won't rain. ....
3 It may rain. ....
4 It's possible that it'll rain. ....
5 It might rain. ....
6 It'll probably rain. ....
7 It probably won't rain. ....
8 It'll definitely rain. ....

a ☂☂☂ = Yes, certain.
b ☂☂ = Yes, more or less certain.
c ☂ = Maybe yes, maybe no.
d ☒☒ = No, more or less certain.
e ☒☒☒ = No, certain.

5 Put the words in order. Then give a percentage of certainty for each, 50, 80 or 100.

1 team the win our Perhaps competition will .
.... = ...%

2 tonight won't It probably cold be .
.... = ...%

3 will finish my homework soon I definitely .
.... = ...%

4 out tomorrow She won't definitely go .
.... = ...%

5 do the They week may exam next .
.... = ...%

6 this My probably call brother will afternoon .
.... = ...%

GRAMMAR CHALLENGE

6 Find and correct nine mistakes in the text.

I'm not feeling very well so I won't definitely go swimming this evening. Mum is made me an appointment and I'll see the doctor this afternoon. He will tell me to stay in the bed – I'm not sure. I'll expect Miss Jones will give back our homework in class tomorrow. May you collect mine for me, please? I definitely will be at home this evening and I'll probable be in bed – so I'll phoning you then.

Developing vocabulary and listening

1 **Look at these possible meanings for *get*. Rewrite the sentences by omitting *get* or *get to* and using the correct form of the words in the box.**

arrive (at) • become • bring • obtain/buy • receive

1 When do you get angry?
   When do you become angry?
2 How many emails do you get a week?
3 What time do you usually get to school?
4 Do you get presents for your parents when it's their birthday?
5 Are you going to get something to eat or drink on the way home after school?
6 Does your bedroom get hot in the summer?
7 What time do you usually get home after school?
8 Do you get tired of watching TV?
9 What did you get for your last birthday?
10 Have you ever got a famous person's autograph?
11 Please get me the pen that's on the table.

2 **LISTENING** ▶ 23 **Listen to the dialogue and answer the question.**
What is the girl's project about?
a how climate change is caused
b how to reduce climate change
c how to deal with climate change

STUDY SKILLS
What's your main objective the first time you listen to a listening text?
➤ STUDY SKILLS page 95

3 ▶ 23 **Listen again and complete the sentences from the dialogue. Use the words in the box to help you.**

annoyed • energy • good signal • homework
information • permission • work • worse

1 Yesterday we .... from Miss Barber.
2 My dad works for a company that looks at different ways of .... from the wind and the sea.
3 The situation is ....
4 They have to .... from people to build wind farms.
5 My dad .... when people refuse.
6 Perhaps your dad can .... and pictures.
7 If I go online where I live, I ....
8 He'll email you some information when ....

🔍 **VOCABULARY EXTENSION**

4 **Match the phrasal verbs (1–5) with their meanings (a–e). Use your dictionary if necessary.**
1 I get up at seven o'clock every day.
2 I get back from school at five o'clock.
3 I got out of the meeting just before lunch.
4 I'm getting behind with my project. I've only done half of it and I need to give it in tomorrow.
5 Why don't we get together at the weekend?

a return
b spend time together
c leave
d leave your bed after sleeping
e do something slower or later than necessary

Grammar in context

1 **Circle the correct alternative to complete the rules.**
   1 We use the zero conditional to talk about *a specific, unique situation/something that is generally true*.
   2 We use the present simple in *one half/both halves* of the sentence.

2 **Match the halves to make sentences.**
   1 If you go online at my house, ...
   2 If you run as fast as you can, ...
   3 If you write too quickly, ...
   4 If you read the newspaper every day, ...
   5 If you look regularly at your vocabulary list, ...
   6 If you work on a computer all day, ...
   7 If you refuse to have wind or solar farms, ...
   a you know what's happening in the world.
   b you don't help the environment.
   c your eyes sometimes hurt.
   d you often make mistakes.
   e you remember words more easily.
   f you don't get a good signal.
   g you get tired very quickly.

3 **Circle the correct alternative to complete the rules.**
   1 We use the first conditional to talk about *possible/impossible* situations and their consequences.
   2 We use *the present simple/will* in the half of the sentence with *if*.

4 **Circle the correct alternative.**
   1 If we *make/will make* changes now, the weather in the future *won't be/isn't* so bad.
   2 She *doesn't/won't* come tonight if you *don't/won't* invite her.
   3 If our car *doesn't/won't* work tomorrow, my dad *takes/will take* it to the garage.
   4 If you *need/will need* help next week, I *come/will come*.
   5 The police *arrest/will arrest* him tomorrow if they *find/will find* evidence.
   6 If you *play/will play* that song again, I *go/will go* mad.
   7 If she *doesn't/won't* play in the next match, her team *loses/will lose*.

5 **Write sentences in the first conditional using the prompts below.**
   1 If/he/have a problem/he/speak to the teacher.
   2 I/go to the doctor/if/my hand/hurt tomorrow.
   3 He/not be happy/if/he/miss the bus.
   4 If/my sister/go to music lessons/my mum/buy her a guitar.
   5 If/you/see the film tomorrow/you/know how the story ends.
   6 The teacher/give me a bad mark/if/I/not give her my homework.
   7 You/not see me/if/you/come late.
   8 If/you/not switch off your mobile phone/people/get angry.
   9 The picnic/be a disaster/if/the weather/be bad.
   10 If/we/not go to the shops/we/not have enough food.

GRAMMAR CHALLENGE

6 **Complete the sentences with the correct form of the verbs given.**
   1 If Michael .... (not come) soon, I .... (go) home.
   2 I .... just .... (see) the weather forecast and it .... (rain) tomorrow.
   3 When I .... (wake) up during the night, the wind .... (blow) very hard.
   4 We .... (go) to the beach on Saturday, but I'm not sure. If my dad .... (not work), we .... (definitely go).
   5 Our class .... (watch) a documentary about climate change next week. The teacher thinks it .... (be) very interesting for us.

Developing speaking

1 **LISTENING** ▶ 24 **Listen and complete the dialogue with the words in the box.**

> about • don't • fancy • great • how
> OK • shall • up

Katie: What are you (a) .... to tomorrow?

Tom: Nothing really. What (b) .... you?

Katie: Nothing planned. Do you (c) .... going to the Planet Earth exhibition in town?

Tom: Sure. What time (d) .... we meet?

Katie: (e) .... about half past ten?

Tom: Fine. Why (f) .... we meet at the bus stop next to my house?

Katie: (g) .... but where shall we meet if it rains?

Tom: Come straight to my house.

Katie: Good idea. I'll see if Amy wants to come.

Tom: (h) ....! See you tomorrow.

2 **Complete the list with phrases from the dialogue.**

Asking about somebody's plans

a ....

b Do you ....?

Arranging to meet

c What time ....?

d ....

e ....

Responding to plans and arrangements

f ....

g ....

h ....

💬 PRONUNCIATION

3 ▶ 25 **Read the questions. Which sentences go up at the end? Listen and check.**

1 What are you up to tomorrow?
2 What about you?
3 Are you up to anything tonight?
4 Where shall we meet?
5 What time shall we meet?
6 Do you like art exhibitions?
7 How about half past ten?
8 Why don't we meet at the bus stop?
9 Do you fancy going to an exhibition?

🔍 DESCRIBING PICTURES

4 **Look at the photo and write your answers to the questions in your notebook. If you're not sure of something, use *I think* and/or *I imagine*.**

1 Who can you see in the photo?
2 Where are they?
3 What are they doing?
4 How do you think the people are feeling? Why?

5 **LISTENING** ▶ 26 **Listen to a student talking about the photo. Complete the text.**

There are two people in the picture. I think they're friends and they're (a) .... together. They're in the (b) .... and it looks very beautiful. In the (c) .... there's a lake or a river and they are cycling on a track going (d) .... it. There are some mountains (e) .... the background and the weather (f) .... very good. The people are perhaps (g) .... a cycling holiday or perhaps they're cycling at the weekend for (h) .... I think they're enjoying the activity. It's good to see lovely countryside and it's good to be (i) ...., too.

6 **SPEAKING** **Now look at the second photo and answer the same questions.**

I can make arrangements Unit 6

Developing writing

1 **Complete the table by putting the linkers in the correct place.**

> Finally • Firstly • Furthermore • However
> Nevertheless • Next • What's more

Sequence	Addition	Contrast

2 **Read the letter in the newspaper. Which reason for objecting to a new airport is not mentioned?**

a pollution
b increased traffic
c cost
d loss of countryside

LETTERS TO THE EDITOR

Not another airport!

Let's make it clear right from the start. The government wants to build a new airport here in the city, but I am totally against the idea. Doesn't the government realise that another airport means more planes, and more planes mean more pollution? That means air pollution and noise pollution. And what about the people who live in the area where they want to build this new airport? How will they live with all this pollution from the sky? And how will they live with all the road traffic that this airport will bring to the area? A new airport? I say NO.

Mr. Jones, London

3 **Complete the sentences from a reader's letter with the correct alternative.**

1 I agree with Mr. Jones. <u>Firstly/However</u>, there will be a lot more pollution from the planes. <u>Next/Nevertheless</u>, life for people who live in the area will be terrible because of the traffic. <u>Next/Finally</u>, if they build an airport like this, it will cost a fortune!

2 Some people say that we need more airports. <u>Furthermore/However</u>, I don't agree with this idea. People don't need to travel so much because we use the Internet to have international meetings and things like that. <u>Next/What's more</u>, we could spend the money that we invest in airports on improving the roads.

4 **Plan a letter to the newspaper about the idea for a new airport. Do not write complete sentences.**

Paragraph 1: *Express your opinion and explain your main reason for it.*

Paragraph 2: *Give an additional reason for your opinion.*

Paragraph 3: *Finish with one final reason for your opinion.*

STUDY SKILLS

Read the letter again. Why is it important to divide texts into paragraphs when we write?
➤ STUDY SKILLS page 95

5 **Write your letter here. Use the linkers from 1.**

Dear Editor,

I am writing in response to a letter about airports which appeared in your newspaper last Wednesday.

Firstly,

Next,

Finally,

I will be interested in hearing other readers' opinions on this question.

Yours faithfully,

Revision: Units 1·2·3·4·5·6·7·8·9·10

Grammar

1 Circle the correct alternative.
1. I don't really know, but Joe *may/will* win the competition.
2. It *won't probably/probably won't* rain tomorrow.
3. They say it *is snowing/is going to snow* tomorrow because it's so cold.
4. The effects *will definitely/definitely will* be terrible.
5. Nobody is certain, but humans *will/might* travel to Mars in around 2050.
6. A: Someone's at the door! B: OK, I *'ll/'m going to* go.

2 Complete the sentences with the first or zero conditional form of the verbs given.
1. If she .... (go) to London, she'll be able to see the London Eye.
2. She won't say anything if you .... (tell) her a secret.
3. If you put snow in your hand, your hand .... (get) cold.
4. If we have the chance, we .... (travel) all around Europe next summer.
5. If you look directly at the sun, it .... (be) bad for your eyes.
6. Sara .... (do) well in tomorrow's exam if she .... (think) carefully.

3 Rewrite the sentences using the word given. Do not change the meaning.
1. Anna might phone later and then we can go shopping together.
   if
2. This is my first visit to France.
   never
3. It's possible that we'll get our results tomorrow.
   might
4. Jack's bag wasn't as expensive as mine.
   more
5. What did your new laptop cost you?
   much
6. We've lived here for two years.
   ago

Vocabulary

1 Put the letters in order to find different geographical features.
1. leungj — j...............
2. trsofe — f...............
3. tesdre — d...............
4. mintoanu grean — m............... r...............
5. lidnas — i...............
6. cabhe — b...............
7. layvle — v...............
8. naceo — o...............

2 Match the words in the box with the definitions. There are more words than definitions.

> drought • flood • global warming • greenhouse effect
> ozone layer • recycle • save • waste

1. when it rains a lot and rivers get too big ....
2. when you save old things to use the materials again ....
3. when you use things in an unnecessary way ....
4. the thing which protects the earth from the sun ....
5. when it doesn't rain and there is no water ....
6. when you stop using something or use very little ....

3 Find a synonym for *get* in these sentences.
1. I'll *get* your bag. ....
2. Can you *get* me a newspaper when you go to the shops? ....
3. She usually *gets* home early. ....

4 Match the sentences (1–5) with the follow up sentences (a–e).
1. I've got stomach ache. ......
2. That book is really informative. ......
3. The film will be repeated tomorrow. ......
4. A man burgled Dad's shop. ......
5. I made a lot of mistakes. ......

a. I learned a lot.
b. I ate too much.
c. I got a bad mark.
d. It's on channel three.
e. The police have got a description.

Gateway to exams: Units 5-6

Reading

1 Read about a cameraman called Matt Howard. Choose the best answers.

LIFE BEHIND THE CAMERA

Matt Howard is a cameraman who works on nature documentaries. He has filmed all over the world in jungles, rainforests and deserts. Here he tells us about his job.

'To film nature documentaries, it's important to be good with a camera, obviously. But, in my opinion, it's more important to be interested in plants and animals. If you aren't, the work can be really boring. To make a two-minute film of a bird, insect or animal, you can sometimes spend a day or a week looking for them. And animals aren't like actors. They don't just appear when you want them to. Sometimes they never appear!'

Matt knows that his job is very important. When he travels to ice caps or deserts, he sees that the environment is changing. His job is to film a world that may disappear one day. 'If the environment continues to change because of global warming, the only place where you'll be able to see some animals and insects is in nature documentaries. I hope our work helps people to understand that we all need to do something to save the planet.'

Generally, changes in technology make Matt's life easier. 'High-definition (HD) cameras help to get better pictures. But if you make a small mistake with an HD camera, it looks much worse than with an old camera. It's true that the new cameras aren't as heavy as the old ones.' But sometimes Matt carries 35 kilos, climbs up a mountain, and tries to film at the same time!

Matt knows what he wants when he makes films. 'I want to film things that people have never seen before. Or I want to film things they've seen, but in a new way. I want it to be a unique experience for the people watching.' In the future, Matt hopes to do more work filming underwater. He thinks this will be very exciting for him and for viewers. New technology is making underwater filming more and more interesting.

And the scariest experience he's ever had? 'We were making a TV programme about polar bears in the Arctic ice cap. We weren't filming at the time, we were sleeping. Suddenly I heard the sound of a polar bear right next to my ear. I was too frightened to open my eyes. It stayed there for five minutes and then left. Believe me, they were the longest five minutes of my life!'

1 Matt says that …
  a he doesn't like his job much because it isn't very exciting.
  b it can take a long time to make a short film.
  c the most important thing in his job is the camera.

2 Matt also says that animals …
  a don't always do what you want.
  b don't like actors.
  c don't like appearing in films.

3 Matt thinks his work is important because …
  a he is protecting some animals, insects and plants.
  b it may be the only way that people can see some animals and insects in the future.
  c he makes programmes about saving the planet.

4 Matt thinks that new HD cameras …
  a always take better pictures than old cameras.
  b are lighter than old cameras.
  c usually take worse pictures than old cameras.

5 Matt …
  a wants people to see something new and different when they watch his work.
  b has done a lot of work underwater.
  c thinks cameramen need more advanced technology.

6 A few years ago Matt …
  a had a frightening experience when a polar bear came too close.
  b became frightened of filming polar bears.
  c couldn't sleep because of the noise polar bears made.

Listening

2 LISTENING  27 Listen to a radio programme where people are giving their opinions about famous people who speak on TV about the environment and other world problems. Match the speakers (1–4) with their opinions (a–e). There is one option that you do not need.

Speaker 1 .... Speaker 3 ....
Speaker 2 .... Speaker 4 ....

a Famous people do a lot of good for environmental problems.
b Generally, the public isn't very interested in environmental questions.
c The most important thing is for people to talk about what they know.
d Famous people are just interested in getting attention for themselves.
e It's better for famous people to give a good example than to tell other people what to do.

The Leonardo DiCaprio Foundation helps protect wildlife.

Use of English

3 Complete the second sentences so that they mean the same as the first. You should use between three and five words, including the word given.

1 I need to read a book at night to get to sleep. **if**

  I don't get to sleep at night .... a book.

2 It's possible that we'll have a test in class tomorrow. **might**

  .... in class tomorrow.

3 I don't earn as much as David does. **than**

  I .... David does.

4 I might come home early and then I can cook dinner. **if**

  I'll cook dinner ....

5 Learning Russian is more difficult than learning French. **as**

  Learning Russian .... learning French.

6 Gary is too young to learn to drive. **enough**

  Gary .... to learn to drive.

7 I've decided to talk to the teacher after the lesson. **going**

  I .... to the teacher after the lesson.

8 The clothes in London are cheaper than the clothes in New York. **more**

  The clothes in New York .... the clothes in London.

COMMON MISTAKES

5 Correct the mistakes in the sentences. In some sentences, there is more than one mistake.

1 I'm not as clever than my sister at maths.

2 This is the more difficult grammar I've ever done.

3 Bye! I'm going to see you later.

4 Do you help me if I can't understand this text?

5 I get headaches if I'll stay in bed too long in the mornings.

6 It wasn't enough warm for sunbathing yesterday, unfortunately.

7 Are you up at anything at the weekend?

8 It might definitely rain later. I'm sure of it.

9 This cake is too tasty. Can I have another piece?

10 We may to go skiing next year. I'd love that.

11 Do you fancy to come round later?

12 I got a good grade for French. That is more, I came top in science.

Writing

4 You recently saw a documentary on television about the environment. Write a review of the programme for your school website. Write about:

- basic information about the programme (title/channel/time of day)
- a description of the programme (mention the environmental issues it talked about)
- why you did or did not like it
- your recommendation

7 Job hunting

Vocabulary

1 Complete the jobs with the missing vowels (*a, e, i, o, u*).

1 r...c...pt.......n...st
2 b......ld...r
3 sh...p .....ss....st....nt
4 m....ch....n....c
5 f....sh......n d....s....gn....r
6 j........rn....l....st

2 Look at the person in the photo. Do you think the sentences about her job are True (T) or False (F)?

1	She works with children.	T / F
2	She works indoors.	T / F
3	She does paperwork.	T / F
4	She does manual work.	T / F
5	She deals with the public.	T / F
6	She travels a lot.	T / F
7	She works with numbers.	T / F
8	She works with a computer.	T / F

3 Find adjectives in the word search and match them with the correct synonym or definition.

K	H	A	Z	L	Z	S	Z	F	N	G	W
X	F	R	M	Q	C	A	R	I	N	G	Z
I	C	M	D	B	R	V	I	O	M	K	C
K	R	R	R	E	I	C	R	L	F	E	L
B	E	M	E	P	J	T	A	D	S	W	E
U	L	T	P	A	S	C	I	G	B	A	V
W	I	K	O	E	T	G	L	O	G	Y	E
P	A	Q	O	X	D	I	K	Z	U	U	R
Y	B	F	W	T	N	F	V	W	W	S	Q
A	L	W	A	W	A	H	I	E	P	I	C
U	E	W	R	I	G	N	K	T	P	C	D
S	O	C	I	A	B	L	E	T	E	K	R

1 with lots of imagination and new ideas ....
2 healthy ....
3 can lift heavy things ....
4 intelligent ....
5 kind, helpful and sympathetic to other people ....
6 a friendly person who likes being with other people ....
7 somebody you can depend on ....
8 somebody who doesn't easily get excited, worried or angry ....
9 somebody who wants to be the best ....

🔍 VOCABULARY EXTENSION

4 Write the nouns for these adjectives.

1 ambitious .... 4 creative ....
2 confident .... 5 strong ....
3 reliable .... 6 fit ....

5 Complete the sentences with nouns from 4.

1 Even with all my ...., I couldn't lift it.
2 You need a lot of .... to stand on a stage and talk to lots of people.
3 My .... is to become a famous singer.
4 If I'm going to run in the marathon, I need to improve my ....
5 My brother is an artist and his paintings show a lot of ....

58 Unit 7 I can talk about jobs, work and personal qualities

Reading

1 Look at the photo. What do you think the animal sculpture is made of? Read the article to check your answer.

   a gold   **b** stone   **c** cheese

A SMELLY JOB?

For most people, cheese is something you should eat to get your calcium. But not for Sarah Kaufmann. Sarah looks at cheese in a completely different way. She is one of a few people in the world who have a very unusual job.
5 Sarah is a cheese sculptor from Wisconsin in the US. Sarah spends her days designing and carving cheese into statues! Sometimes these sculptures are enormous, like a 137-kilo gorilla she once created, or quite small – she also makes little sculptures, like violins, for weddings or other special
10 events.

But how did she get such an unusual job in the first place? It's not the most common option when students are thinking about a career! Sarah was always an artistic child and she did an art course at college when she left school.
15 She eventually became the creative director of a dairy company and she employed people to carve cheeses. She thought it would be a good way to promote the cheeses. Then, she decided to have a go at doing the sculptures herself and found she loved it. Sarah started carving cheese
20 in 1981. By 1996, her sculptures were so popular that she had to give up her regular job and start sculpting cheese full time. Now she travels all over the world creating cheese sculptures for food fairs, supermarkets and other special events.

25 Carving cheese is not an easy job. Sarah has to first design the sculpture on paper. Then she must enlarge the drawings and copy them to make the sculpture. If it's very large or complicated the work might take up to ten days to finish! Sometimes she has to do this in front of an audience
30 and she mustn't make a mistake. But Sarah rarely does. She's very good at her work. We imagine that a sculpture made of cheese won't last very long but surprisingly one of these can last up to seven or eight weeks. Of course it shouldn't be in a warm place. Sarah's cheese of choice
35 for sculpting is Wisconsin cheddar because it's quite hard and salty and it doesn't have to be in a fridge. It's also very tasty. Sarah sometimes works long hours – 10 to 12 hours sculpting, but she keeps going. She doesn't have to stop work to eat either, because she can just eat the cheese!

40 But why do people make sculptures out of cheese? Apparently, it's all about educating and informing people of the benefits of eating cheese – an unusual form of advertising! But, it's much more interesting than a TV advert about cows and farms, isn't it? If I had the chance,
45 I would love to try it! There's another professional job connected with carving food into sculptures and that's butter sculpture. Now, that might be a little more difficult!

2 Read the article again and decide if the statements are True (T) or False (F). Write down the number of the line where you found the answer.

1. Sarah creates sculptures of different sizes.   T / F ....
2. Sarah wasn't interested in art when she was young.   T / F ....
3. She has worked as a full time cheese sculptor since 1981.   T / F ....
4. She became a cheese sculptor by chance.   T / F ....
5. Sarah only works in the US.   T / F ....
6. It sometimes takes Sarah ten days to finish even a simple sculpture.   T / F ....
7. Sarah quite often makes mistakes when she's carving in front of other people.   T / F ....
8. Cheese sculptures last longer than we think they do.   T / F ....
9. Sarah creates cheese sculptures to encourage people to eat cheese.   T / F ....

3 🛠 **CRITICAL THINKING**

Which of the statements are facts (F) and which are opinions (O)?

1. Cheese sculptures can last a long time in the right conditions.   F / O
2. Cheese sculpture is more interesting than a TV commercial.   F / O
3. There aren't many cheese sculptors in the world.   F / O
4. Cheese sculpture is a form of advertising.   F / O
5. Butter sculpture is more difficult than cheese sculpture.   F / O
6. Wisconsin Cheddar is a good cheese for making sculptures.   F / O

4 Match the underlined words in the article with the definitions.

1. an artistic object that you make by shaping different material   ....
2. make bigger   ....
3. cutting a shape   ....
4. opportunity or possibility   ....
5. try something   ....
6. choice   ....
7. a mineral in cheese that is good for bones   ....
8. an area of work that you choose for your future   ....

I can understand an article about a job   Unit 7

Grammar in context

1 Read the sentences and choose the alternative which describes the meaning of the sentence.
1 Wisconsin Cheddar doesn't have to go in the fridge. *obligation/no obligation*
2 Sarah has to enlarge the drawings. *obligation/prohibition*
3 You should eat cheese to get calcium. *recommendation/obligation*
4 A cheese sculpture doesn't have to be very big. *no obligation/prohibition*
5 You must try your best. *obligation/prohibition*
6 You shouldn't leave cheese in a warm place. *prohibition/advice*
7 You mustn't get distracted when you're carving. *no obligation/prohibition*

2 Write complete sentences using the prompts below and the correct form of *have to* or *don't have to*.
1 Normally teachers/wear a uniform.
2 Normally a firefighter/wear a uniform.
3 I/go to school on Sunday.
4 A receptionist/know how to use a computer.
5 Builders/wear hard hats.

3 Complete the sentences with *must* or *mustn't*.
1 You write carefully in exams.
2 People make a lot of noise inside hospitals.
3 Students use mobile phones in class.
4 Professional musicians practise playing their instrument.

4 Complete the sentences with *should* or *shouldn't*.
1 People use violence to solve their problems.
2 You take medicine when you aren't ill.
3 You help your friends when they have problems.
4 When you're bad at something, you practise to get better.
5 People switch off their mobile phones in the cinema.

5 Circle the correct alternative. Sometimes two are correct.
1 Children *has to/have to/don't have to* go to school.
2 You *must/mustn't/don't have to* copy in exams.
3 Doctors *must/mustn't/have to* work hard.
4 You *has to/have to/must* wear smart clothes if you work in a bank.
5 Hospital visitors *mustn't/must/don't have to* talk in a loud voice or shout because it is prohibited.
6 You *must/don't have to/mustn't* use a mobile phone in a petrol station.

GRAMMAR CHALLENGE

6 Find and correct a mistake in each sentence.
1 Children under 15 must to go to school.
2 This exercise is optional – you mustn't do it.
3 If you'll break the rules, you'll get punished.
4 You should to do extra work if it's difficult.
5 Students haven't to wear a uniform in our school and so you can wear what you want.
6 If you have to doing it now, I'll help you.
7 You musn't drink and drive – it's illegal.
8 You don't have to open the car door when the car is moving.
9 You should eat chocolate just before you go to bed because it isn't good for your teeth.

Developing vocabulary and listening

1 Complete the crossword.

Across

1 He's the first person to arrive at work and the last person to go. He does more than anybody else. He's very hard-................. .

4 They're a very attractive couple. She's very beautiful and he's good-................. .

6 You've got the pen in your left hand. Are you left-................. ?

8 She's the director of a large multinational company. I'm sure she's well-................. .

Down

2 You should be more relaxed and easy-................. .

3 That teacher only teaches two lessons a day. He's part-................. .

5 She's well-................. . She always knows where she should be and what she has to do.

7 People from Northern Europe sometimes have blonde hair and are blue-................. .

STUDY SKILLS

How do you learn new vocabulary? Which do you think is better: revising for a long time just once before an exam or revising for a shorter period more frequently?
➤ STUDY SKILLS page 95

2 LISTENING 28 Listen to the dialogue between two friends and answer the question.

What is the main focus of their discussion?

a which job is best paid
b what they should study at university
c what jobs their family members do

3 28 Listen again and decide if they agree (A) or disagree (D) about these things.

1 They have to make the right decision now. A / D
2 The boy should study computer science. A / D
3 A well-paid job is important. A / D
4 The girl should study drama. A / D
5 Acting is badly-paid. A / D

VOCABULARY EXTENSION

4 Match these words to make compound adjectives. Then match them with the definitions (a–f). Use your dictionary if necessary.

1 self-   dressed
2 open-   fashioned
3 well-   reliant
4 bad-   minded
5 old-   respected
6 well-   tempered

a open to new ideas and different opinions ....
b not modern ....
c people have a good opinion of you ....
d you get angry often or quickly ....
e able to do things for yourself and not depend on other people ....
f wearing good clothes ....

5 Complete the sentences with the compound adjectives from 4.

1 She's very ...., but that's because she spends all her money on clothes.

2 I like him because he's very .... He listens to you and thinks before he says yes or no.

3 She's very independent and .... She doesn't think her parents have to do everything for her.

4 My older brother is so .... He always shouts at me, and for no reason!

5 She's a .... writer. Lots of people have bought her books and admire her work.

6 I think she's quite .... All her clothes are long and look like my grandmother's clothes!

Grammar in context

1 **Match the halves to make sentences.**

1 If you were good at computer science,
2 If I were an actor,
3 I'd study that course
4 If I had a summer job,
5 I'd change my job

a I would enjoy every day.
b I'd have to get up early in the holidays.
c if it were shorter.
d if I didn't enjoy it.
e that would be a great choice.

2 **Look at the sentences in 1 and decide if these rules about the second conditional are True (T) or False (F).**

1 The second conditional talks about improbable and imaginary situations. T/F
2 The second conditional talks about past situations. T/F
3 We use *would* in the half of the sentence with *If*. T/F
4 We can use *was* or *were* with *If I/he/she*. T/F
5 The half of the sentence with *If* always comes first. T/F

3 **Circle the correct alternative.**

1 If you *aren't/weren't* my brother, I'd be really angry.
2 If it was hot all year, I *won't/wouldn't* go out.
3 If I *were/am* you, I'd buy a new mobile phone.
4 If they *didn't/don't* have a pet, they'd be able to go away in the summer.
5 We *would/will* enjoy the concert more if we knew the songs.
6 They *would/will* continue running if they didn't get tired.
7 I'd do what he said if he *was/is* my boss.
8 TV would be better if there *aren't/weren't* any adverts.
9 If I *could/can* sing, I'd start a band.
10 If you went out more, you *won't/wouldn't* be lonely.

4 **Complete the sentences with the second conditional form of the verbs given.**

1 If I .... (have) a problem, I'd call you.
2 If the bus didn't come, we .... (walk).
3 I .... (not be) happy if my parents didn't let me go out.
4 You wouldn't learn much if you .... (play) computer games all day.
5 If you .... (learn) to speak a new language, it would help you find a job.
6 If John was faster, he .... (play) football better.
7 They'd leave the restaurant immediately if they .... (not like) the food.
8 If I knew the answer, I .... (tell) you.
9 If I .... (find) money in the street, I'd try to find out who it belonged to.
10 I'd buy that coat if I .... (have) enough money.
11 If I were you, I .... (ask) the teacher to explain the homework again.

GRAMMAR CHALLENGE

5 **Rewrite the sentences using the words given. Do not change the meaning.**

1 It's a good idea to stay at home and revise this evening. **should**

.... and revise this evening.

2 It isn't necessary to give this homework in tomorrow. **have**

We .... this homework in tomorrow.

3 Eating in class isn't allowed. **we**

.... in class.

4 I'd like to be rich and go round the world. **if**

.... round the world.

5 My advice is to go to bed early. **if**

.... to bed early.

6 You should buy your mum a present to say thank you. **would**

If I .... to say thank you.

7 It's too cold to go to the beach today. **enough**

It's .... to the beach today.

8 Apples are healthier than crisps **not**

Crisps .... apples.

Unit 7 I can use the second conditional

Developing speaking

1 Put the words in order to make polite requests.

1 me you starts Can tell job when the ?

2 if I need Could you any ask experience ?

3 you tell me apply how Could I can ?

4 we you do me tell to what have Can ?

5 Could the wages I ask what are basic ?

6 you me tell Can address your what is ?

2 Complete the dialogue with the requests from 1.

A: Good afternoon?

B: Good afternoon. I'm calling about a job that was in the newspaper yesterday. Could I ask for some information?

A: Certainly.

B: Thanks. **(a)** ....

A: Yes. It begins on 1st July and it finishes on 31st July.

B: Oh, I see. **(b)** ....

A: Well, you have to give some sports lessons in the morning, and in the afternoon you take children on excursions.

B: I see. **(c)** ....

A: It's not essential, but we prefer people who've done similar work before.

B: I understand. **(d)** ....

A: It's £250 a week, and lunch is included.

B: **(e)** ....

A: You just need to send us a letter of application and CV.

B: That's great. **(f)** ....

A: Yes, it's …

💬 PRONUNCIATION

3 ▶ 29 Read the questions and circle the words you think are stressed. Listen and check. In the questions is *can* pronounced with /æ/ or /ə/?

1 Can you tell me when the job starts?
2 Could I ask if you need any experience?
3 Can you tell me how I can apply?
4 Can you tell me what we have to do?
5 Could I ask what the basic wages are?
6 Can you tell me what your address is?

➕ DESCRIBING PICTURES

4 Look at the photo and write your answers to the questions in your notebook. If you're not sure of something, use *I think* and/or *I imagine*.

1 Who can you see in the photo?
2 Where are they?
3 What are they doing?
4 How do you think the people are feeling? Why?

5 LISTENING ▶ 30 Listen to a student talking about the photo. Complete the text.

There are four people **(a)** .... the photo. Three of them are sitting **(b)** .... a table in a restaurant and they are ordering a meal. The waitress is writing **(c)** .... their order. I think it's lunchtime **(d)** .... they're wearing summer clothes that you wear **(e)** .... the day time. I think the waitress is a student in her summer holidays. **(f)** .... she wants to earn some extra money. I think the people at the table are feeling happy because **(g)** .... they've been shopping and they're having a break. They're **(h)** .... hungry, too! The waitress doesn't look very busy **(i)** .... she's probably enjoying her job. It's not a very well-paid job, but **(j)** .... you are good, the customers leave you tips.

6 SPEAKING Now look at the second photo and answer the same questions.

STUDY SKILLS

What should you do if you notice you are making mistakes when you are speaking?

➤ STUDY SKILLS page 95

Developing writing

1 Read the letter of application on the right. What type of job do you think Benjamin wants?
   a teaching tennis to adults
   b organising tennis competitions
   c organising sports and games for children

2 Circle the correct alternative in the letter on the right.

3 Put these headings in the correct place in the CV.
   1 Interests
   2 Education and qualifications
   3 General information
   4 Work experience

CURRICULUM VITAE
Benjamin Martin

(a) ....
1 .... 12 Sefton Street, Sunderland, SU7 8BV
2 .... (mobile) 0567 123 4567/ (home) 651 10 11 12
3 .... benmart@binter.com

(b) ....
Summerfield School, Sunderland
(GCE) A-levels in English Literature, French and Economics

(c) ....
JULY 2013
Worked at Foxton Tennis Club giving lessons to 5–10 year olds
JULY 2015
Worked at Knightley Tennis Club as assistant

(d) ....
Tennis
Reading
Good knowledge of computers

4 Now put these specific titles in the correct place in the CV.
   a Address:
   b Email:
   c Telephone:

5 Take a piece of paper and write out your own CV. Use the completed CV on this page as a model.

12 Sefton Street
Sunderland
SU7 8BV
7th February 2015

(a) *Dear/Hi* Ms Nicholson,

I am writing (b) *in/for* response to your advertisement in The Birmingham Sun. (c) *I'd/I would* like to apply (d) *at/for* the job which you advertised in this newspaper on 5th February. I (e) *give/enclose* a CV with information about myself, including education and work experience. (f) *Like/As* you will see, tennis is one of my main hobbies. I have (g) *experience/interest* of giving tennis lessons and of working with children. I also think that I am patient, (h) *good/well*-organised and (i) *hard/fast*-working.

I look forward to (j) *hearing/hear* from you.

(k) *Yours sincerely/Love from*,

Benjamin Martin

6 Read the advert and write a letter of application for the job.

Do you have some free time in the summer holidays and want to earn some money?

We are looking for three young people to be guides on our tour buses of the town. You will need to be interested in history and able to speak another language.

Send a letter of application with your CV to Norris Tours, 3 Church Lane, Southford, SU64 7FD

Revision: Units 1·2·3·4·5·6·7·8·9·10

Grammar

1 **Complete the sentences with *doesn't/don't have to* or *mustn't*.**

1 I .... finish this homework before Monday so I can relax now!
2 You .... park there because it's where the headteacher parks his car.
3 We .... wear a uniform.
4 My dad .... give me a lift to college because I've got my own car now.
5 I .... go to bed late tonight because I start work early tomorrow.
6 Kay .... be late again today.

2 **Complete the sentences with the correct form of *should, have to, will, might*.**

1 I .... apply for college next week, but I don't know which subjects I .... choose.
2 It .... rain later so you .... take an umbrella just in case.
3 If I don't get this job, I don't know what .... happen. My dad says I .... worry, but I do!
4 I .... fill in a job application. Can you help me?
5 My sister .... get up early for her new job. But I .... get up until 9.30!

3 **Complete the sentences with the correct form of the verbs given.**

1 If my brother .... (come) home late I always .... (wake up), even if he .... (be) very quiet.
2 I .... (go) to university if I .... (get) the right grades in my exams next month.
3 I .... (not work) in an office even if you .... (pay) me an enormous salary!
4 If I .... (not have) a job I .... (sit) at home and watch daytime TV all day.
5 It's my birthday next month. If I .... (have) a party, ... (you help) me organise it?

Vocabulary

1 **Complete the sentences with the correct jobs.**

1 There's water coming through the ceiling! Call a ....
2 The car won't start. We need a ....
3 We want a new wall in the garden. Dad's employed a ....
4 When you get to the hotel speak to the ....
5 I want to change this shirt I bought yesterday so I'll talk to the ....
6 Our cat isn't very well so we have to take him to the ....

2 **Match these words to make compound adjectives. After each compound adjective, say if it describes a person (P) or a job (J).**

| going • handed • looking • paid • time • working |

1 hard-............... P / J   4 right-............... P / J
2 easy-............... P / J   5 good-............... P / J
3 part-............... P / J   6 well-............... P / J

3 **Complete the adjectives about personal qualities with the missing vowels (*a, e, i, o, u*).**

1 ...mb...t.......s   4 s...ns...t...v...
2 c...nf...d...nt   5 f...t
3 cr.......t...v...   6 cl...v...r

4 **Complete the sentences with the correct adjectives.**

1 Connor enjoys looking after other people. He's very c............... .
2 Jacquie never gets worried, she always remains c............... .
3 I love going out and meeting other people. I'm s............... .
4 You can depend on me to do everything you ask. I'm r............... .
5 Mollie expected to get 90% in her test, but she only got 50%. She's d............... .
6 Mark fell over during the football match. His leg is b............... .
7 I've got a cold and my throat is very s............... .
8 I was so sad at the end of the film that I cried. It was very m............... .

Grammar and vocabulary revision Units 1–7 65

8 Best friends forever

Vocabulary

1a Match the phrases in the box to the pictures.

> fall out • hang out with somebody
> make up • see eye to eye

1 ....

2 ....

3 ....

4 ....

1b Match the phrases in the box with these sentences.

> circle of friends • get on well
> have a lot in common • have an argument

1 My sister and I never argue, even though we're very different. ....

2 Jack and I always spend the weekends together because we like doing the same things. ....

3 I got really angry with Sarah when she told me she didn't like my shoes. ....

4 Pete, Sam, Ben and Rob have been friends since primary school. ....

2 Complete the comments with the correct form of the phrases from 1.

1 My brother and I don't .... about anything! We have very different opinions.

2 Jack .... with Mandy. She told the teacher that he copied her work and now he won't speak to her.

3 I've got a new friend and we .... For example, we both love sports and scary films!

4 I've .... with Harry after our argument. I said I was sorry and now everything's OK!

3 Complete the puzzle by writing the noun form of each adjective. Is the word in the shaded column positive or negative?

1 angry   3 excited   5 happy
2 bored   4 afraid   6 lonely

```
         s
¹a  n  g  e  r
       ²
   ³
          ⁴
      ⁵
   ⁶
```

VOCABULARY EXTENSION

4 Write the nouns for these adjectives.

1 confused ....
2 relaxed ....
3 stressed ....
4 embarrassed ....
5 disappointed ....
6 depressed ....
7 worried ....
8 surprised ....

5 Complete the sentences with the nouns from 4.

1 We didn't know what to do. There was a lot of .... after the accident.

2 There's always .... if you have to cancel a trip.

3 .... at weekends is very important if you have a stressful job.

4 Beth gives her parents a lot of .... when she doesn't tell them where she's going.

5 I got a car for my birthday. It was an amazing ....!

Unit 8 I can talk about friendship and feelings

Reading

1 Read the title of the web article and answer the question. Then read the article to check your answer.

What do you think the article is about?
a the qualities of a good friend
b the end of a friendship
c how to make good friends

Best friends forever??

A really good friend can be as important in your life as a brother or sister and sometimes even more! But what happens when a friendship goes wrong? Read a post to our website from reader Emily Carter.

Lucy is my best friend and has always been there for me – at least, she used to be. Lucy and I met at primary school on our very first day. We sat next to each other that day and every day for the next ten years! We became really close friends and we used to do everything together. We had lots of things in common – we liked the same music, the same sports, the same TV programmes. We used to share all our problems and there was always someone to complain to when I didn't see eye to eye with my parents. I thought we'd be best friends forever.

Last month everything changed. Lucy texted me one evening and I will never forget the message. She wrote: 'Our friendship is over. I never want to speak to you again.' I couldn't believe it. OK, we'd had lots of arguments over the years – everyone does – but we'd never said anything like this. I felt completely lost and confused.

Then I realised what had happened and I felt very stupid. Lucy and I had argued about clothes the day before. We had both said nasty things. It wasn't a big argument, it was really silly. But after we had had the argument, I did something really stupid. I was feeling angry, so I emailed a friend and said some nasty things about Lucy. But then, I made a mistake and clicked the wrong icon on my computer screen and sent the email to everyone in my address book. By the time I realised my mistake, everyone had read the nasty message. Of course, Lucy's text message meant that Lucy had read the email, too. She hasn't spoken to me since that day.

So, our friendship is over. I've apologised again and again but she still refuses to speak to me. I can understand. In one silly moment I destroyed our relationship. There's a lot of advice for people who are having different kinds of problems, but no one thinks about how bad it feels when a friendship breaks up. I feel very lonely, very guilty and very sad. Can you help?

STUDY SKILLS

To do the next exercise, you will need to read the text in a different way from exercise 1. How and why?

➤ STUDY SKILLS page 95

2 Read the article again. Choose the best answers.
1 When did Lucy and Emily become friends?
  a when they started secondary school
  b through doing the same sport
  c at the beginning of their education
2 Why was Emily confused when she got Lucy's text?
  a She couldn't remember having an argument.
  b Their argument hadn't been very important.
  c She didn't realise it was from Lucy.
3 Why was Lucy upset?
  a Because Emily said nasty things during their argument.
  b Because Emily wrote nasty things about her.
  c Because Emily sent her a nasty text message.
4 Which is true about the email?
  a It was an accident.
  b It was a joke.
  c It was unavoidable.
5 Why do you think people write to this website?
  a to get advice about problems
  b to tell interesting stories
  c to complain about their relationships

3 **CRITICAL THINKING**

Which two opinions are expressed in the text?
1 There should be more advice for people whose friendships break up.
2 Friendships are never stronger than family relationships.
3 You have to have a lot in common to be good friends.
4 Friendships cannot last forever.
5 You need to be careful when you send an email.

4 Match the underlined words from the text with the definitions.
1 a picture or word on your computer screen ....
2 a bad feeling when you feel you've done something wrong ....
3 tell each other ....
4 finished ....
5 damaged something very badly so it cannot be normal again ....
6 not very nice ....

I can understand an article about friendship   Unit 8   67

Grammar in context

1 **Circle the correct alternative to complete the rules.**
   1 We form the past perfect with had + *present/past* participle.
   2 We use the past perfect when we talk about actions that happened *before/after* another action or actions in the past.

2 **Which two time expressions do we not use with the past perfect?**

   after • as soon as • by the time
   recently • when • while

3 **Match the halves to make sentences. Then <u>underline</u> the thing which happened first in each sentence. Is the verb in the past simple or the past perfect?**
   1 After we had had the argument ......
   2 By the time I realised my mistake ......
   3 She started reading a new book ......
   4 They hadn't eaten anything all day ......
   5 When they had had their dinner ......
   6 He didn't swim ......
   7 They had won the competition ......

   a they washed the dishes.
   b so they had a party to celebrate.
   c I did something stupid.
   d because he had forgotten to bring his towel.
   e so they ordered a big pizza.
   f I had sent the nasty message.
   g because she had finished the one she was reading.

4 **Look at these important dates in history and write positive or negative sentences with the past perfect.**
   1 4500 BC – invent the wheel ✓
   By 4500 BC they had invented the wheel.
   2 1400 – start to print books ✗
   ......
   3 1805 – make the first battery ✓
   ......
   4 1895 – discover X-rays ✓
   ......
   5 1900 – fly for the first time ✗
   ......
   6 1910 – discover penicillin ✗
   ......
   7 1932 – split the atom ✓
   ......
   8 1953 – find the structure of DNA ✓
   ......
   9 1960 – walk on the moon ✗
   ......

5 **Complete the rule with the correct ending.**
   We use *used to* to talk about:
   a something we couldn't do in the past, but we can now.
   b something that we liked doing in the past, but not now.
   c something that we did regularly in the past, but we don't do now.

6 **Complete the sentences with the correct form of *used to*.**
   1 We .... to share all our problems.
   2 We didn't .... to go to the same school but we do now.
   3 Did you .... to go to the same school as Emily?

7 **Complete the sentences and questions using the correct form of *used to* and the verbs in the box.**

   go • have • live • take • walk • watch

   1 I .... in the countryside when I was young.
   2 I .... for lots of walks in the forest with my friends.
   3 We .... a lot of TV because we were always outside.
   4 .... to school in the mornings?
   5 My dad .... me to school by car.
   6 We .... school on Wednesday afternoons – those afternoons were free!

GRAMMAR CHALLENGE

8 **Find and correct ten mistakes in the story.**

   Danny is playing tennis every Saturday with his friend Jordan. One Saturday, they started playing at 12 o'clock and by 5.30, they played five whole games. After they were finished the last game, Danny had a shower and went home. But his back and neck had really hurt. He was a bit worried. Maybe he injured his back during the tennis game. When he was younger his neck wasn't hurting after tennis. Perhaps he must visit the doctor. Danny decided to have a long hot bath and then go to bed. Luckily, when he had got up the next morning, his pain went. It wasn't been anything serious after all. Next Saturday he would play six games!

Developing vocabulary and listening

1 **Put the letters in order to make nouns. Then complete the table by writing the nouns in the correct column.**

edmofer • slilens • moredob • snakewes • dessans
massend • redpinfish • peashspins • illensones
tinshiporeal • dimgonk • pridesalhe

-ness	-ship	-dom
		freedom

2 **Complete the sentences with the adjective or noun form of the words from 1.**

1 You don't look well. Are you _ill_? Do you need a doctor?
2 I have a good .... with my sister. We get on well.
3 After ten years in prison they finally let him out and gave him back his ....
4 Why are you so ....? Have you won the lottery or something?
5 She hasn't got any brothers or sisters or any good friends. I think she's .... with nobody to talk to.
6 I'm quite .... I'm not strong enough to put the bags up there.
7 Your .... is really important to me. We've been friends since we were five.
8 You look like you are going to cry. Why are you so ....?
9 People weren't happy with the president's ....
10 I like reading a book to stop ....
11 Queen Elizabeth I ruled her .... for 45 years.
12 My friends think I'm .... for spending so much money on clothes. They think I should save up.

3 **LISTENING** ▶ 31 **Listen to a boy talking about his best friend. Who is Betsy?**

a a class mate
b a dog
c someone who lives near him

4 ▶ 31 **Listen again and complete the notes.**

Notepad
1 Zac is a .... year-old boy.
2 Eight years ago he had a serious ....
3 As a result he couldn't go back to ....
4 Because of this, Zac had a problem with .... and ....
5 Now Zac has a .... Labrador called Betsy.
6 Betsy can have some .... in the park to run around.
7 Eating too many .... is not good for Betsy.
8 Betsy can sense when Zac is feeling ....

VOCABULARY EXTENSION

5 **Match the nouns (1–8) with their definitions (a–h).**

1 darkness   5 awareness
2 wisdom   6 tiredness
3 blindness   7 partnership
4 hardship   8 stardom

a knowledge and understanding of a situation
b black, without much light
c after a lot of activity
d this comes from having a lot of experience and knowing a lot
e inability to see
f difficulties in your life
g being very famous
h two or more people doing an activity together

STUDY SKILLS

What things can you do outside the class to improve your listening?

➤ STUDY SKILLS page 95

Grammar in context

1 Match the rules (1–7) with the sentences (a–g).
1. We use the gerund as the subject of a sentence.
2. We use the gerund with *go* to talk about physical activities.
3. We use the gerund after verbs of liking or disliking.
4. We use the gerund after prepositions.
5. We use the infinitive to explain why somebody does something.
6. We use the infinitive after adjectives.
7. We use the infinitive after certain verbs.

a My classmates love hav**ing** a dog in the class.
b I'm good at do**ing** maths.
c I want **to go** out by myself.
d I couldn't go shopp**ing** on my own.
e I went home **to see** if my mum was OK.
f Go**ing** to school was difficult, too.
g It's hard **to stop** giving Betsy biscuits.

2 Match the halves to make sentences.
1. Professional football players should enjoy
2. Last week my grandfather and I went to Wembley Stadium
3. Scoring goals is important
4. It's important for football players
5. Professional football players don't often go
6. For professional football players, it usually isn't good

a to train hard.
b to eat lots of burgers because they aren't very healthy.
c skiing because they could have an accident.
d for football players.
e to watch a football match.
f playing football.

3 Complete the questions (1–8) and answers (a–h) with the correct form of the verbs given.

1 What do you enjoy .... (do) on Saturday afternoons?
2 How often do you go .... (shop) with your friends?
3 .... (do) sport. How important is it for you?
4 What are you good at .... (do) at school?
5 How do you feel about .... (read) in English?
6 What do you want .... (do) when you finish school?
7 Do you find it easy .... (make) new friends? Why/Why not?
8 What do you hate .... (do) at the weekend?

a Chemistry. .... (do) tests and experiments is really fun.
b I like it but it's difficult .... (know) all the words.
c Going to the cinema with my friends. I enjoy .... (see) new films.
d Very. I love .... (play) tennis and I go .... (swim) once a week.
e Usually once a week after school. We spend a lot of time .... (look) and not much money .... (buy)!
f I'd like .... (become) an artist. I love .... (paint) and .... (draw).
g Not really. .... (get) to know new people is always difficult .... (do).
h .... (clean) my room. It is *so* boring but my mum always expects me .... (do) it before .... (go) out.

4 Match the questions and answers from 3.

GRAMMAR CHALLENGE

5 Find and correct eight mistakes in the story.

Every Saturday my friends going into town to watching football. I don't enjoy to watch sports so I usually go to the library while they're in the stadium. Then we meet up afterwards to having a pizza. Last Saturday, they persuaded me going with them because it was an important match. Unfortunately, it started to raining and we haven't brought our umbrellas. It was terrible. Next week, I will going to the library again – no more football for me.

Unit 8 I can use the gerund and the infinitive

Developing speaking

1 **LISTENING** ▶ 32 **Listen to the dialogue and answer the question.**

How did Nick's family celebrate his brother's birthday?

a They had a party.
b They went to France.
c They went for a meal.

2 ▶ 32 **Complete the information using the correct form of the verbs in the box. Listen again and check.**

> x2 be • eat • have • know
> organise • start • work

1 Tony's birthday .... on Saturday.
2 His parents .... a meal at The Hotel on the Park.
3 His friend's aunt .... there.
4 The meal .... at 7.30.
5 There .... 20 people at the celebration.
6 Nick .... most of the people.
7 Nick .... fish in a sauce.
8 While they .... coffee Nick and Tony's dad made a speech.

3 **SPEAKING** Imagine that last Saturday you went to a birthday celebration. Talk about it for a minute. Record your answer. Use these questions to help you.

1 What was the celebration?
2 Where was it?
3 Who did you go with?
4 Did you know everyone?
5 What happened?
6 Did you enjoy the event? Why/Why not?

PRONUNCIATION

4 ▶ 33 **Look at the phrases and mark if the intonation goes up or down at the end. Listen and check. Then repeat for practice.**

1 How fantastic!
2 Did you know anyone?
3 What a surprise!
4 He's at university, isn't he?
5 That's brilliant!
6 I love it!

DESCRIBING PICTURES

5 **Look at the photo and write your answers to the questions in your notebook. If you're not sure of something, use *I think* and/or *I imagine*.**

1 Who can you see in the photo?
2 Where are they?
3 What are they doing?
4 How do you think the people are feeling? Why?

6 **LISTENING** ▶ 34 **Listen to a student talking about the photo. What are his answers to the questions?**

7 **SPEAKING** Now look at the second photo and answer the same questions.

I can report a past event Unit 8 71

Developing writing

1 Read the email from Grace and answer the question.

What is Grace's problem with her friends?
a They always pay for her.
b They don't have much money and she does.
c She spends too much when she's with them.

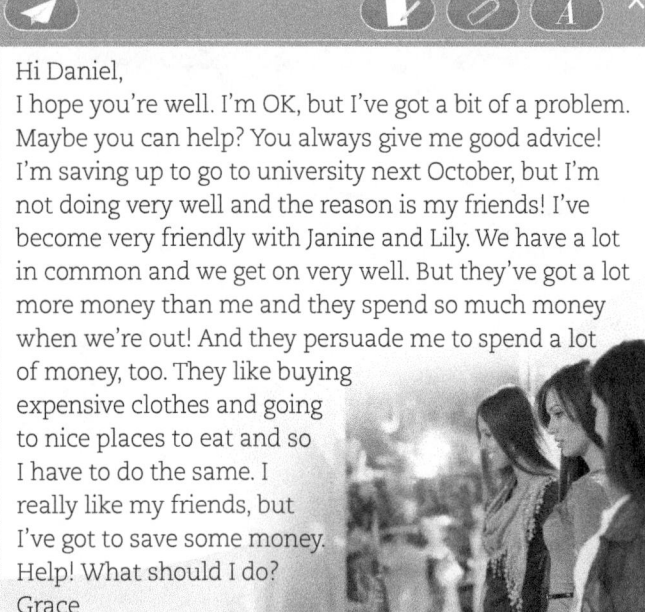

Hi Daniel,
I hope you're well. I'm OK, but I've got a bit of a problem. Maybe you can help? You always give me good advice! I'm saving up to go to university next October, but I'm not doing very well and the reason is my friends! I've become very friendly with Janine and Lily. We have a lot in common and we get on very well. But they've got a lot more money than me and they spend so much money when we're out! And they persuade me to spend a lot of money, too. They like buying expensive clothes and going to nice places to eat and so I have to do the same. I really like my friends, but I've got to save some money. Help! What should I do?
Grace

2 Read Daniel's reply and put phrases 1, 2 and 3 in the correct places in the email.

Hi Grace,
I'm sorry you're having problems.
Here are some ideas. First of all **(a)** .... They probably don't realise. Once they know that it's very important for you, they will understand why you can't buy a lot of clothes or eat expensive meals. You say that they're nice people, so I'm sure they will understand. Next, **(b)** .... People like being able to help. So, ask them to stop you from spending too much money! Tell them that when you're out together shopping and you are going to buy something you don't need they should say 'Stop!' Lastly, **(c)** .... That doesn't mean you have to stop hanging out with them. You can still go to the park or do sports together. If they really are good friends they will know that this is the right thing for you to do.
I hope that's helped a bit! Let me know how you get on,
Daniel

1 you should spend less time in shops with them for a while.
2 you need to ask them to help.
3 I think you have to tell them that you need to save money and that you're trying very hard not to spend too much.

3 Which expressions could replace the following?
1 First of all ....
2 Next ....
3 Lastly ....

4 You have received this email from your cousin. Read the email and tick (✓) which things you should mention in your email in reply.

Hi Andrew,
I hope you're still enjoying life in the US. I need to ask you for some advice.
My best friend is called Luke. I've known him for about five years. We've always done everything together. Last month some new students joined our class and now Luke is spending lots of time with them. He never asks if I want to hang out with them. He never answers my texts or emails. Or, if he does, he just says something short like – see you later. We used to see each other every evening after school to chat or play computer games. Now I'm really lonely. I don't know what I've done wrong and why he wants to hang out with them. He's only just met them! I feel really bad and I can't concentrate on studying for my exams. I just don't know what to do. Any ideas?
Matt

1 Matt must concentrate – exams important for the future ☐
2 he should talk to Luke about the problem ☐
3 perhaps this interest in new friends will pass ☐
4 he could invite Luke and his new friends round for an evening ☐
5 he needs to find a new friend himself ☐

5 Write your email to Matt to give him some advice. Remember to use expressions of sequence and time.

Revision: Units 1·2·3·4·5·6·7·8·9·10

Grammar

1 Decide which action happened first and put one verb in the past perfect and the other in the past simple.

1 I got up/I made my breakfast
   After ....
2 he finished his lunch/he wasn't hungry
   When ....
3 she got out of the swimming pool/she swam for 20 minutes
   When ....
4 I sent the email/I wrote it
   After ....
5 I had a shower/I played tennis
   After ....
6 I put on my pyjamas/I went to bed
   After ....
7 we caught the bus home/we watched the film at the cinema
   After ....

2 Use the correct form of *used to* and the verbs given to complete the sentences.

1 I .... (enjoy) dancing, but recently I've done quite a lot and it's fun.
2 .... he .... (live) near you? I know that now he's moved to Glasgow.
3 I'm sure our summers .... (be) much warmer than they are now.
4 This room .... (be) the kitchen, but Dad's built a new room on the house and we use that as a kitchen now.
5 Kathy .... (like) Ben, but now they're best friends.

3 Complete the sentences with the words in the box.

doing • to do • swimming • to swim watching • to watch

1 .... sport is good for you.
2 It's important .... your homework every day.
3 I enjoy .... cartoons and dramas.
4 I got up early .... the news on TV.
5 Are you good at ....? Can you put your head under the water?
6 Do you want .... in the sea this afternoon?

Vocabulary

1 Complete the sentences with the correct words or phrases.

1 I used to have a much bigger .... of friends.
2 My sister and I had an ...., but now we've .... up.
3 I don't see .... with my parents about my choice of clothes.
4 Do you .... with your brothers and sister?
5 I'm not going to Oliver's party because I've .... with him.

2 Write the nouns which describe these feelings.

1 the feeling when you aren't happy = ...
2 the feeling when nobody is with you = ...
3 the feeling when you are afraid of something = ...
4 the feeling when you've got nothing to do = ...
5 the feeling when you are angry = ...

3 Write the nouns we can make from these words.

1 excited .... 5 weak ....
2 friend   .... 6 ill   ....
3 relation .... 7 leader ....
4 free   .... 8 mad   ....

4 Complete the words and phrases.

1 .... father = your mother's new husband
2 .... throat = when your throat hurts and you can't speak, for example
3 shop .... = stealing from a shop
4 .... show = a TV programme with a competition, often to win money
5 mountain .... = a line of mountains like the Andes
6 global .... = the change in the temperature around the world

Grammar and vocabulary revision Units 1–8 73

Gateway to exams: Units 7–8

Reading

1 Read the article about child labour and decide if the statements are True (T) or False (F). Write the number of the line where you found the answer.

A difficult childhood

Most teenagers in Europe have busy lives. They work hard at school, then maybe they do after-school activities or sport, they go out with their friends, and sometimes they do a Saturday job. But don't forget that there are approximately
5 218 million children in the world between the ages of five and 17 who have to work almost every day of the year.

There's a big difference between a job at the weekend in a supermarket and the type of jobs that these young people have to do. Working in a supermarket is an example
10 of child work. Child work is an economic activity which isn't bad for a child's health or education. But the other is what we call child labour. That is when children work in dangerous conditions. Right now millions of children are working in mines, or working with chemicals and pesticides
15 in agriculture, or working with dangerous machines in factories. These children not only work in bad conditions. They also work very long hours. Often they get no money for their work.

Of the 218 million children in child labour around the
20 world, the majority (69%) work in agriculture. They work in very high temperatures and they use dangerous equipment like knives or machetes. Their working conditions are dirty and unhealthy. They have to work long hours and so at the end of the day they are very tired. But that's when they
25 have to be most careful because, if not, they can suffer fatal accidents. And you should also remember that these children don't usually receive any medicine or medical treatment.

So, why do so many young children have
30 to work in these terrible conditions? The reason is because of poverty. Their parents need money for their families to survive and the children have to help get this money. It's not usually big companies
35 that force children to work – it's their parents. Another common reason is the terrible lack of schools in many areas. The children can't go to school because there isn't one. Or it might be
40 a long way from where they live or even too expensive for the children to go to. So, instead of going to school, the children go to work.

So next time you think that your life
45 is difficult, remember that there are people of your age in worse conditions. We should all think about doing something to help them. There are already
50 laws, but people don't always follow them. So, more laws wouldn't help. However, if there were more free schools, that might
55 make a big difference to the lives of these children.

1	The writer believes that some children have much more difficult lives than others.	T / F ……
2	Child labour is any work that a child under 17 does.	T / F ……
3	The writer believes that it is always bad for children to work.	T / F ……
4	Many children do not receive any wages.	T / F ……
5	Most of the dangerous work that children do is on farms.	T / F ……
6	Usually it is big companies that make the children work.	T / F ……
7	Often children work because they are not able to get an education.	T / F ……
8	The writer believes that new laws would not be helpful.	T / F ……

Listening

2 **LISTENING ▶ 35** Listen to two students talking about university. Choose the best answers.

1 Sophie's university lectures …
   a start too early.   b start at the same time every day.
   c never start before 10.30.

2 Sophie sometimes misses her lectures …
   a because she's got too much work to do.
   b because she can't get up in the morning.
   c because she doesn't have to go to them all.

3 Sophie is living …
   a in a flat on her own.   b with her aunt and uncle.
   c with some other students.

4 Sophie is probably …
   a sociable.   b hard-working.   c shy.

5 She knows someone who …
   a has good technological skills.
   b is studying computer science.
   c loves cooking.

6 Ben wants to visit so that he can …
   a cook for Sophie.   b see her flat.
   c get to know some of her friends.

Use of English

3 Read about how to choose a career. Choose the best answer (A, B, C or D) to complete the text.

Choosing a career is a decision that is very difficult (1) .... Some students don't really know a lot about the different jobs that they can do or what work is really like. (2) .... some work experience before you (3) .... to make a decision is often a good idea. Before Mark Owen decided to become a teacher he (4) .... already spent a short time helping in a local primary school as part of the work experience programme at his school. He thinks he learned a lot from (5) .... this and he believes that everyone should have the chance. If all schools arranged some work experience for their students, it (6) .... benefit them a great deal. 'I (7) .... that teaching was an easy job,' says Mark. 'But after my work experience I realised that it definitely isn't! You (8) .... follow a career if you don't know exactly what it means.'

1	A	making	B	make	C	to make	D	for making
2	A	Getting	B	Get	C	Do get	D	Have got
3	A	should	B	must	C	have	D	going
4	A	has	B	had	C	was	D	did
5	A	to do	B	do	C	doing	D	done
6	A	will	B	should	C	would	D	can
7	A	was thinking	B	used to think	C	have thought	D	think
8	A	don't have to	B	wouldn't	C	don't have to	D	shouldn't

Writing

4 Write a letter to apply for the job in the advert. Include this information. You can invent it.
- Why are you writing?
- What other information are you sending with the letter (CV, photo, other)?
- What personal qualities and experience do you have that could help to do the job?

JONES' NEWSAGENT'S
We need a hard-working teenager to deliver newspapers this summer.

Write to Mr L.T. Jones, 36 Atlantic Drive, Bristol, B06 3LP, or ring 07984 231786.

⚠ COMMON MISTAKES

5 Correct the mistakes in the sentences. In some sentences there is more than one mistake.

1 As soon as I have finished my work I went out.

2 I didn't used to like reality TV shows, but I do now.

3 Learn another language takes a long time.

4 Do you enjoy to work in an office?

5 Firstly of all, I think you should to go to the doctor.

6 Are you interesting to come to the museum with me?

7 Hi Mr Brown, I'd like to apply to the job you advertised in the newspaper.

8 I mustn't go to the dentist for another year!

9 If I would have enough money, I'll travel around the US. But I don't have any!

10 You don't have to eat that chocolate! It's isn't good for you.

11 We used to living in the town centre.

12 When I opened my bag I saw that someone stole my money.

9 Bestsellers

Vocabulary

1 Find different types of fiction in the word search. Write them next to the different titles (1–11).

1. Macbeth
   The Importance of Being Earnest ....
2. X-Men
   Spiderman ....
3. Frankenstein
   Dracula ....
4. Harry Potter and the Philosopher's Stone
   The Lord of the Rings ....
5. Love Story
   The Notebook ....
6. Stormbreaker
   Casino Royale ....
7. Cinderella
   Snow White ....
8. The Mysterious Affair at Styles
   The Adventures of Sherlock Holmes ....
9. The Time Machine
   War of the Worlds ....
10. Batman: The Dark Knight Returns
    V for Vendetta ....
11. The Book Thief
    The Other Boleyn Girl ....

E	O	W	F	I	I	T	T	C	P	Y	D	Z	A	X	N	F
C	Y	W	H	T	M	L	M	T	L	X	W	E	P	O	Q	A
M	A	T	C	I	X	H	G	Q	A	R	C	T	I	R	H	I
R	Q	K	S	T	Y	O	E	S	Y	N	F	T	J	W	Y	R
G	O	C	A	D	S	R	Y	X	A	C	C	R	G	S	F	Y
C	T	J	O	U	Y	R	Y	M	Y	I	J	V	A	O	T	T
O	O	W	X	Z	M	O	O	L	F	W	I	T	J	T	Y	A
M	Q	B	Q	N	P	R	Q	E	M	U	N	H	C	I	L	L
I	N	J	P	A	C	M	C	D	A	A	F	Q	M	J	X	E
C	V	X	T	W	Y	N	Y	Z	F	F	I	O	L	P	G	Y
A	S	S	B	U	E	T	H	R	I	L	L	E	R	Y	Y	R
F	R	C	R	I	M	E	N	O	V	E	L	Q	M	I	O	Q
A	Y	W	C	G	R	A	P	H	I	C	N	O	V	E	L	D
H	I	S	T	O	R	I	C	A	L	F	I	C	T	I	O	N

3 Match each type of non-fiction book (1–8) with the type of information it gives (a–h).

1 atlas ....   5 guidebook ....
2 autobiography ....   6 manual ....
3 cookbook ....   7 newspaper ....
4 encyclopaedia ....   8 magazine ....

a how to find a place and what you can do there
b ingredients for a dish and how to prepare them
c the geographic location of different places
d what has happened very recently
e how to use or operate something
f about the writer's life
g about almost anything in the world
h reports, photos and stories, usually weekly or monthly

2 Look at these fictional characters. Choose the type of book in 1 that each one comes from.

1 a fairy

2 an alien

3 a superhero

4 a musketeer

5 a princess and a frog

6 a detective

⊕ VOCABULARY EXTENSION

4 Complete the sentences with the words.

> acts • articles • chapter
> contents • scene • headline • index

1 I looked up the subject in the .... at the back to find out which page it was on.
2 My dad cuts out newspaper .... about our village to keep in a special book.
3 The .... on the front page said: Big Crash.
4 The .... page said it had three parts.
5 I knew who the thief was after reading the first ....
6 The play was long – there were five ....
7 I love the .... at the end of the play.

Unit 9 I can talk about fiction and non-fiction

Reading

1. Look at the photograph and the title of the article and answer the question. Read the article to check.

   What do you think a cell phone novel is?

   a a book about cell phones
   b a book that is written on a cell phone
   c a book that teaches people how to write

The cell phone novel

Has new technology changed our reading habits? (1) .... Although paperbacks remain the most popular form of book that we buy, e-books have become extremely popular. Amazon, the big online company, recently said that they sell more e-books than physical books now. It is very easy to download a new novel to your e-reader and carry it with you everywhere. (2) ....
Have you heard of the cell phone novel?

Ten years ago in Japan something new and exciting happened. When texting became a popular way to communicate in 2000, students in Japan started to use their phones to write stories, too. (3) .... They created a new art form which also became very popular and companies created websites where readers could download new chapters and interact with the writers. Cell phone novels were very different from normal books. The chapters were very short and dramatic – only about 200 words long. (4) .... They added new chapters when they (or their readers) wanted them to. Often the novels were published later as physical books and even became films or TV series. This way of writing was exciting because it meant that everyone with a mobile phone could write and people across the world could read their work.

Today the cell phone novel has become popular in the English language, too. (5) .... In a recent interview he said that the cell phone book was a combination of poetry and story-telling. This is because the chapters are so short, and the writers must be very imaginative when they use words. The stories are dramatic and emotional and they are usually about relationships and feelings.
(6) ....
Takatsu says that cell phone novels are important because they reflect popular youth culture today and this kind of novel is an art form for the modern technological age.

In Takatsu's opinion, the cell phone novel has encouraged a whole new generation to read and write books. Let us know what you think.

2. Read the article again and put these sentences into the gaps (1–6) in the text.

   a Also, the writers didn't plan the stories.
   b They can also be about worrying topics like bullying.
   c The answer has to be 'yes'.
   d They wrote very short chapters and sent them to readers as text messages.
   e Satoshi Takatsu is the author of the most popular English-language cell phone novel in the US, *Secondhand Memories*.
   f But technology hasn't only changed the way that we read books, it is changing the way people write them, too.

3. **CRITICAL THINKING**

   Which of the statements do you think are advantages of cell phone novels (A), which are disadvantages (D) and which are both (B)?

   1 People have to wait for the next chapters.   A / D / B
   2 People who don't usually read books like cell phone novels.   A / D / B
   3 People might not read classical literature any more.   A / D / B
   4 Everyone can be a writer.   A / D / B

4. Match the underlined words from the article with these definitions.

   1 full of excitement ....
   2 show ....
   3 communicate ....
   4 two or more things together ....
   5 a group of people in society who are born around the same time ....

   STUDY SKILLS

   What do you think is the best thing to do with new words when you read a book in English for pleasure?
   ➤ STUDY SKILLS page 95

5. Complete the sentences with the words from 4.

   1 Today's .... read much less than their parents.
   2 My bad exam results didn't .... how much revision I did – I studied really hard!
   3 Encyclopaedias usually have a .... of pictures and text.
   4 It is important to .... with other students when you are learning English.
   5 The final scene of *Romeo and Juliet* is very ....

Grammar in context

1 Circle the correct alternative to complete the rules about reported speech.

1 When the reporting verb (*say/tell*) is in the past, the tense of the verb in reported speech usually *stays the same/goes one tense back*.

2 When we use *tell* we *must/mustn't* use an object. When we use *say* we *must/mustn't* use a personal object.

3 In reported speech pronouns and possessive adjectives often *change/do not change*.

2 Complete the sentences in the table.

Direct Speech	Reported speech
1 'I write novels.'	He said he ....
2 'I'm writing a novel.'	He said he ....
3 'I have written a novel.'	He said he ....
4 'I wrote a novel.'	He said he ....
5 'I had written a novel.'	He said he ....
6 'I will write a novel.'	He said he ....
7 'I can write a novel.'	He said he ....
8 'I may write a novel.'	He said he ....
9 'I must/have to write a novel.'	He said he ....

3 Decide if the words given are necessary in the sentence or not. If they are necessary, write them in the correct place.

1 My friend said I could use his bike. (me)

2 They told they wanted to go home. (us)

3 The teacher told they had an exam. (the students)

4 He said it was his birthday. (him)

5 He said it wasn't his book. (me)

6 She told she wanted to go shopping. (her mum)

7 I said she was my favourite writer. (the teacher)

8 They told the exam was on Friday. (James)

4 Complete the sentences with the correct words.

1 'I love that film,' said Megan.
Megan said .... that film.

2 'We're going by bus,' said Danny.
Danny said .... going by bus.

3 'That's my bike,' said Jacob.
Jacob said that .... bike.

4 'My dad needs help,' said Olivia.
Olivia said .... dad .... help.

5 'It's late.' said Sam and Ben.
Sam and Ben said it .... late.

5 Rewrite the sentences in reported speech.

1 'I'm going to start playing basketball next month,' said Jamie.

2 'My friend has got a new computer game,' said Jack.

3 'We finished school last Friday,' said Emily and Evie.

4 'I think this is the answer,' said Charlotte.

5 'We don't need help,' said the students.

GRAMMAR CHALLENGE

6 Rewrite the sentences using the words given. Do not change the meaning.

1 'Oliver, you have to be more careful,' said the teacher. **told**
The teacher .... be more careful.

2 'We had lunch at that restaurant last week,' said Ray. **where**
Ray said that .... lunch the previous week.

3 'It's not a good idea to work too late at night,' she said. **I**
She said that ....

4 'If it's sunny tomorrow I'll walk to school,' said my friend. **following**
My friend said that if it was sunny .... walk to school.

Developing vocabulary and listening

1a Match the words to make phrasal verbs.

1	cross	a	over
2	read	b	in
3	flick	c	out
4	read	d	out
5	fill	e	up
6	turn	f	through
7	look	g	on

1b Write the full phrasal verb beside the correct definition.

1 continue reading ....
2 turn a page to see the other side ....
3 turn through the pages of a book quickly ....
4 read so that other people can hear you ....
5 try to find a particular piece of information in a book ....
6 draw a line through something to show it isn't correct ....
7 write information in empty spaces ....

2 Circle the correct alternative.

1 In some exercises you have to fill *in/on* the gaps.
2 He wrote *wich* but then he crossed it *out/up* and wrote *which*.
3 I don't know this word. I need to *look/read* it up in my dictionary.
4 We've finished this page. Turn *on/over* to the next one.
5 I'm going to *flick/turn* through this magazine quickly to see if I can find any good photos.
6 Read *on/out* the answer in a loud voice so that we can all hear you.
7 I really want to know how this story ends, so I'm going to read *out/on*.

3 LISTENING ▶ 36 Listen to three people talking about reading and writing and answer the question.

Which question do you think the people are answering?

a How has reading and writing changed in recent years?
b Is reading and writing quicker to learn these days than in the past?
c Does your parents' generation have problems reading and writing online?

4 ▶ 36 Listen again. Which speaker mentions …

1 making mistakes? ....
2 looking up words? ....
3 filling in forms? ....
4 turning over pages? ....
5 crossing out words? ....
6 flicking through books? ....
7 looking up information? ....

5 ▶ 36 Decide if the statements are True (T) or False (F). Listen and check.

1 Speaker 1 likes using a dictionary. T/F
2 Speaker 1 sometimes looks up information online. T/F
3 Speaker 2 makes a lot of mistakes in his essays. T/F
4 Speaker 2 uses computers to do his written schoolwork. T/F
5 Speaker 3 often reads an e-book while travelling. T/F
6 Speaker 3 likes touching the pages of a real book. T/F

VOCABULARY EXTENSION

6 Match the phrasal verbs (1–4) with their meaning (a–d). Use your dictionary if necessary.

1 read up on ....
2 sum up ....
3 note down ....
4 dip into ....

a read only small parts (of a book, for example)
b write something down to remember it
c give a summary of something
d get information on a subject by reading a lot about it

7 Complete the sentences with the correct form of the phrasal verbs from 6.

1 Have you got a pen? You can .... my address.
2 I didn't read all of the book. I just .... it to see if I liked it.
3 I need to .... Ancient Rome for our test next week.
4 In the last paragraph of your essay, it's a good idea to .... the main ideas.
5 In lessons, the teacher explains and we .... the most important points in our notebooks.

I can understand people talking about reading and writing   Unit 9   79

Grammar in context

1 Look at the direct and reported questions (a–c) and decide if the rules are True (T) or False (F).

a	'What did you do differently at school?' Sarah asked her mum. Sarah asked her mum what she had done differently at school.
b	'Which article are you reading?' Gabby asked Ben. Gabby asked Ben which article he was reading.
c	'Do you look up lots of things online?' David asked Harry. David asked Harry if he looked up lots of things online.

1 We don't change tenses and pronouns in the same way in reported statements and reported questions.   T / F
2 We don't use question marks in reported questions.   T / F
3 We use the auxiliary verb *do* in reported questions.   T / F
4 We don't put the verb before the subject in reported questions.   T / F
5 We use *if* or *whether* in reported questions when there is no question word (*who, what, why*, etc.) in the original question.   T / F

2 Rewrite the questions in reported speech.

1 'Are you sure about this answer?' the teacher asked the boy.
   The teacher ....

2 'Why are you crying?' the girl asked the boy.
   The girl ....

3 'Is it your birthday today?' Beth asked Nathan.
   Beth ....

4 'Do you know the time?' Adam asked Mia.
   Adam ....

5 'Where have you put my glasses?' Eric asked his granddaughter.
   Eric ....

6 'How did you know my name?' William asked the girl.
   William ....

7 'Have you read this book?' Sophie asked Tom.
   Sophie ....

8 'Do you like crime novels?' Mark asked Sally.
   Mark ....

9 'Do you have to wear a uniform to school?' Kate asked Hannah.
   Kate ....

3 Correct the mistakes in the reported questions.

1 'Do you like vanilla ice cream?' Jamie asked Becky.
   Jamie asked Becky whether did she like vanilla ice cream.

2 'Are you listening to this programme?' my mum asked me.
   My mum asked me if you're listening to this programme.

3 'Where does Daisy live?' asked Isabel.
   Isabel asked where Daisy did live.

4 'Why isn't your mobile phone working?' Jack asked Emma.
   Jack asked Emma why wasn't her mobile phone.

5 'Do we need our books today?' the students asked the teacher.
   The students asked the teacher if they needed their books today.

6 'Why are you looking at me?' Amanda asked Pete.
   Amanda asked Pete why was he looking at her.

7 'Did you enjoy the meal?' the waiter asked the customers.
   The waiter asked the customers they had enjoyed the meal?

GRAMMAR CHALLENGE

4 Write the dialogue that Emma and the teacher had in direct speech.

1 The teacher asked me if I was tired.
   Teacher: ....

2 I told her that I was, because I'd watched a late film the night before. I asked her why she had asked that.
   Emma: ....

3 She said that I looked pale. She asked me why I had watched until so late. She said that I shouldn't watch late films on school nights.
   Teacher: ....

4 I told her that she was right, but I'd needed to watch that film. I had had to write a review of it for my English teacher.
   Emma: ....

5 She said she understood, but next time I should record it. Then I could watch it earlier in the day.
   Teacher: ....

6 I told her that next time, I would record it.
   Emma: ....

Developing speaking

1 **LISTENING** ▶ 37 Complete the expressions. Then listen to a short presentation about a book and tick (✓) the ones you hear.

A page from *The Wind in the Willows* by Kenneth Grahame

1 I'm going to .... about … ☐
2 I'd like to begin .... saying … ☐
3 First of .... … ☐
4 What's .... … ☐
5 It's also .... that … ☐
6 Last but not .... ☐
7 Another .... is that … ☐
8 To .... up ☐

2 Which of the statements are good (G) or bad (B) advice about giving a presentation?

1 It's important to write your presentation out fully. G / B
2 Always give a clear introduction and conclusion. G / B
3 Present your points in the order that you think of them. G / B
4 Make sure you read your presentation carefully to the audience. G / B
5 Finish as soon as possible. G / B
6 Look up at the audience from time to time. G / B

💬 PRONUNCIATION

3 ▶ 38 Look and underline the stressed words in the phrases. Listen and check. Then repeat for practice.

1 I'd like to begin by saying that …
2 Last but not least …
3 It's also true that …
4 Another thing is that …
5 To sum up …

➕ DESCRIBING PICTURES

4 Look at the photo and write your answers to the questions in your notebook. If you're not sure of something, use *I think* and/or *I imagine*.

1 Who can you see in the photo?
2 Where are they?
3 What are they doing?
4 How do you think the people are feeling? Why?

5 **LISTENING** ▶ 39 Listen to a student talking about the photo. Complete the text.

Well, there are a few people and they're in a (a) .... On the (b) .... and in the foreground, there is a young woman. I imagine she's a (c) .... She's wearing (d) .... clothes. On the left there's an (e) .... man. They're all looking at books from the shelves. I think it's a bookshop and not a (f) .... because the people are (g) .... up. In a library they would (h) .... down to look at the books. I imagine these people are (i) .... through some books before they (j) .... if they want to buy them. The people are reading and they look quite (k) .... I think they are (l) .... hard because they want to know if the book is a (m) .... one for them to buy.

6 **SPEAKING** Now look at the second photo and answer the same questions.

Developing writing

1 Put the paragraphs of the story in the correct order.

A ☐

(a) ...., Mr. Bird felt a hand on his arm. The tall man who was standing behind him used one hand to pull at his black briefcase. He (b) .... his other hand right in the middle of Mr. Bird's back. And he pushed.

B ☐

It was (a) .... and it was raining when Mr. Bird left his office to go home. He was careful to remember his (b) ...., black briefcase. He smiled. It was full of important papers and it made Mr. Bird feel important, too. He hurried along the dark, (c) .... pavements to the tube station. His (d) .... shiny shoes nearly slipped on the steps as he went down to the platform to wait for the train. He was late and his wife was going to be angry – again.

C ☐

Mr. Bird heard the loud noise of the train coming from the black entrance to the tunnel. There was a rush of cold wind and then the train appeared. The lights in its carriages were shining (a) .... Mr. Bird could see that it was (b) .... full. There were people standing. Their faces were against the glass windows. Mr. Bird stepped forward.

D ☐

The station was very crowded, but he (a) .... pushed his way to the edge of the platform and was ready to jump first into the carriage when the doors opened. He (b) .... the tall man behind him when he left the office. That man (c) .... right behind him now.

2 Complete the story with the words and phrases in the box.

> big • brightly • completely • hadn't noticed • placed
> quickly • six o'clock in the evening • smart
> Suddenly • was standing • wet

3 You are going to write the next part of the story. Look at the pictures and write a short paragraph for each one. Remember these things to make your story interesting.

1 Use adjectives and adverbs.
2 Use different past tenses.
3 Use words and expressions of time and sequence.

STUDY SKILLS

What can you do to practise your writing in English?
➤ STUDY SKILLS page 95

Unit 9 I can write a story

Revision: Units 1·2·3·4·5·6·7·8·9·10

Grammar

1 Rewrite the underlined words as they would appear in reported speech.

1 'It's <u>my</u> birthday,' said Katie. ....
2 'I was in London <u>last week</u>,' said Cameron. ....
3 '<u>Today</u> is going to be a good day,' said Owen. ....
4 '<u>I've</u> been to Africa twice,' said Mark. ....
5 '<u>I</u> wanted to go out last weekend,' said Lucy. ....
6 'The exam is <u>tomorrow</u>,' said the teacher. ....

2 Circle the correct alternative.

1 Ella asked the boy what *your/his/her* name was.
2 The teacher asked her students *that/whether/how* they wanted to see the concert.
3 Ava asked Henry where *is he/was he/he was* going.
4 The doctor asked him if he *has ever had/had ever have/had ever had* a serious accident.
5 Jack asked Isabella if she *liked/does like/did like* that music.
6 Harry asked who *saw/did see/had seen* the film.

3 Rewrite the sentences in reported speech.

1 'I found the information on this website,' said Nick.
   ....
2 'Are you going to see the new film tomorrow?' Angela asked Lynn.
   ....
3 'Where have you been?' the teacher asked Kerry and Liz.
   ....
4 'Did you go to Dave's party yesterday?' Sonya asked Ryan.
   ....
5 'I haven't finished reading your book yet,' Alice said to Mike.
   ....

4 Circle the correct alternative.

On Sundays I always enjoy **(a)** *to watch/watching* a TV documentary series about nature. I **(b)** *saw/have seen* every programme in the series since it **(c)** *started/has started* in 2008. The presenter is a really interesting man **(d)** *who/whose* name is Jack Wild. He doesn't always give **(e)** *many/much* information about the different things they show, but there are **(f)** *any/some* cool scenes with animals that you **(g)** *aren't usually seeing/don't usually see* on TV.

Vocabulary

1 Complete the words for different types of books.

1 a................y
2 f............ t........
3 c................k
4 s.............. f..............
5 m............l
6 p......y

2 Choose the best type of book from 1 for each person.

1 Sam wants to learn how to make a new pasta dish. ....
2 Sophia likes stories about robots. ....
3 Ryan wants to learn how to use his new digital camera. ....
4 Jasmine is four years old and she likes stories about princes and princesses. ....
5 Edward likes reading about the lives of famous people, written by the person him or herself. ....
6 Ben loves the theatre and he loves reading the story again at home. ....

3 Circle the correct alternative.

1 When a story is good, you want to read <u>on/out</u> to the end.
2 When you make a mistake, you cross it <u>on/out</u>.
3 When you want to get a quick idea of a book, you <u>flick/turn</u> through it.
4 At the end of an essay it's a good idea to sum <u>on/up</u> your ideas and opinions.
5 If you don't know how to pronounce a word you should look it <u>over/up</u> in a dictionary.

4 Match the words (1–8) with the endings (a–h) to make nouns. Change the letters where necessary.

1 free   a -ion
2 happy   b -y
3 confident   c -ence
4 burglar   d -dom
5 teach   e -ment
6 collect   f -ship
7 retire   g -er
8 relation   h -ness

10 Log on

Vocabulary

1 Complete the words.

1 ....y....a....d: we use this to type on
2 ...o......t....r: like a television, electronic device with a screen
3 ...e....c....m: we use this so people in other places can see what we're doing
4 ...p....k......: sound comes through this
5 ...r....t......: we use this to produce paper copies of things from our computer
6 ...I...s..... dr........: we use this to save files. We can carry it around with us.
7 ...c........n......: we use this to create electronic copies of paper documents
8 ...o....s...: we use this to move the arrow around and click on things on our computer screens

2 Match the halves to make questions.

1 Have you got **fast** ....
2 Do you ever **chat** ....
3 Which **search** ....
4 How long do you spend **surfing** ....
5 How often do you **down** ....
6 Which **web** ....
7 Do you **read** or **write** ....
8 Do you often use **social** ....

a **load** films from the Internet?
b **site** do you visit the most?
c **online** with friends?
d **the Net** at the weekend?
e **engine** do you usually use?
f **broadband**?
g **a blog**?
h **networking sites**?

3 Complete the comments with words or phrases from 2.

1 I often .... to my friends in other countries.
2 We bought my grandfather a tablet computer and now he regularly .... to find out about fishing and new TV programmes!
3 We've got ...., but the connection is very slow so it sometimes takes me ages to get online.
4 I often .... music that I like from the Internet.
5 In my opinion, ... sites are important for people to keep in contact with friends from around the world.
6 While my brother was travelling last year he wrote a .... and we could see what he'd done every day.

🔍 VOCABULARY EXTENSION

4 Match the phrases to the pictures.

a b c d AVENIR MYRIAD Brush Script
e www f
g _ □ × h INSTALL NOW

1 attach a file ....
2 scroll up and down ....
3 change the font ....
4 insert an emoticon ....
5 bring up a menu ....
6 type in a website address ....
7 install software ....
8 close a window ....

Reading

1 Look at the title of the article and the photo and answer the question. Read the article to check.

What do you think the article will be about?

a a man who stole money from banks using computers
b a man who stole information from companies using computers
c a man whose business was stealing mobile phones

Crime or hobby?

Nowadays, we rely on computers for all parts of our lives, from work to keeping in touch with friends. However, these benefits inevitably lead to dangers. We are regularly reminded how important it is to protect our computers from people who want to use the information on them. Another main target for these criminals, or hackers, is the large companies who keep a lot of confidential information on computers.

One of the most famous hackers in the world is Kevin Mitnick. He began hacking when he was just 15 – he found a clever way to use the buses without paying. More than twenty years later, in 1999, he was arrested and convicted because he had hacked into big company computers and copied software. Mitnik spent more than five years in prison.

There is some controversy about this. Some people believe that the US government over-reacted. They say that he didn't need to go to prison for so long and that his crimes were not that serious. Mitnick says that he did the hacking as a hobby – like most hackers in those days. It was a challenge and hackers did it for the adventure, too. Governments at that time did not really understand the new technology and were very scared of it. Mitnick gives an example. When he was in prison, he was put in solitary confinement for eight months, where he could not see or speak to any other prisoners. This was because officials were worried that he could use the prison phone to start a nuclear war – just by whistling into it!

When he was released from prison, Mitnick was not allowed to go online for a long time. However, after this he began working with computers again – as a consultant for computer security. Now big companies go to him to make sure that their computers are secure and well-protected.

Mitnick believes that computer hacking has changed a lot since he used to do it. He used to do it for fun, but today computers are hacked for profit and this is very dangerous. The hackers are often never found. In his business today, Mitnik gives advice to individuals as well as big companies. His concern is that because there is so much information available today, the hackers will always be able to beat antivirus software.

2 Read the article again and choose the best answers.

1 In the first paragraph we are told that …
   a people don't know about the risks to computers.
   b people worry too much about the risks to computers.
   c people are often told about the risks to computers.

2 Kevin Mitnick thought that hacking into computers …
   a was exciting and enjoyable.
   b was a good way to make money.
   c was a way to get a job.

3 Some people believe that the US government …
   a gave Mitnick the wrong punishment.
   b put the wrong person in prison.
   c didn't discover all his crimes.

4 What does Mitnick do today?
   a He hacks into computers secretly.
   b He is employed to hack into computers officially.
   c He doesn't use computers any more.

5 Mitnick's opinion is that …
   a hackers today have a different attitude to his.
   b hackers today aren't as good as he was.
   c hackers today can't keep up with the advances in technology.

STUDY SKILLS

Why is it important and useful to guess difficult words from their context?

➤ STUDY SKILLS page 95

3 **CRITICAL THINKING**

Are the following statements fact (F) or opinion (O)?

1 Mitnick was given an unfair punishment. F / O
2 People hack into computers to commit crimes. F / O
3 Mitnick didn't use computers after prison. F / O
4 Mitnick could start a war from prison. F / O
5 Hackers will always be ahead of security. F / O
6 Mitnick spent a period of his life in prison. F / O

4 Match the underlined words from the article with these definitions.

1 software that protects a computer ....
2 have contact with friends ....
3 making music or a noise by pushing air through your mouth ....
4 found guilty of a crime ....
5 something that is secret ....
6 something people disagree about ....
7 be more worried than necessary ....

I can understand an article about computer crime Unit 10

Grammar in context

1 Circle the correct alternative to complete the rules about the passive.
1. To make the passive we use the verb *to be* and the *past simple/past participle*.
2. To introduce the person who does the action we use *by/for*.
3. We use the passive when we are more interested in *the action/the person who does the action*.

2 Complete the sentences with an appropriate word.
1. Websites .... used by many students who are learning English.
2. Today computers .... hacked for profit.
3. Hackers are often never ....
4. The iPad is made .... Apple.
5. This television series .... watched in many different countries.
6. The French language is .... in France, Belgium, Switzerland, Senegal and other countries.

3 Circle the correct alternative.
1. These computers *is/are* made in China.
2. A lot of mineral water is *drank/drunk* in the summer.
3. Portuguese is *speak/spoken* in Brazil.
4. The students in my class *are written/write* essays once a month.
5. A lot of rice *is/are* eaten every day.
6. My sister *does/is done* the shopping on Saturdays.
7. German *teaches/is taught* at my school.
8. That song *sings/is sung* on special occasions.
9. New roads *is/are* built each year.
10. My friends *send/are sent* emails to each other every day.

4 Complete the sentences with the present passive form of the verbs in the box.

check • drive • make • play • teach • wear • write

1. Jeans .... all over the world.
2. This sport .... every weekend.
3. On computers, many documents .... by using Microsoft Word.
4. Paella .... with rice.
5. Maths .... in almost all schools.
6. Your passport .... at the airport before you get on the plane.
7. Buses .... by bus drivers.

5 Rewrite these active sentences in the present passive form. Only use *by* plus the agent if you know exactly who does the action.
1. BMW make the new MINI.
2. Sometimes they find gold in this river.
3. They don't stop football matches if it rains.
4. They give a prize to the best actor.
5. In this hotel they take your bags to your room.
6. They don't grow tea in Scotland.
7. In Japan students clean the classrooms.
8. A lot of people use public transport.

GRAMMAR CHALLENGE

6 Find and correct the mistakes in the sentences.
1. The city of Florence is visited for thousands of people every day.
2. Tennis played by two or four players.
3. Many products made in China nowadays.
4. More manga comics are drawing in Japan than in any other country.
5. Sometimes spectacular sunsets is seen in this part of the world.
6. More ice creams eaten in the summer than in the winter.
7. Kevin asked me did I like cars that are made in Japan?
8. Fruit what is sold in markets is often fresher than in supermarkets.

Developing vocabulary and listening

1 Find eight words which frequently go with *email*.

F	A	D	E	R	E	P	L	Y
O	D	W	V	N	U	F	D	A
R	D	L	P	B	N	C	E	D
W	R	T	A	O	S	R	Y	E
A	E	L	M	U	P	I	U	L
R	S	E	R	N	D	F	W	E
D	S	A	C	C	O	U	N	T
Q	W	B	V	E	K	L	B	E
A	S	E	N	D	A	C	C	O
F	O	R	D	C	H	E	C	K

2 Complete these sentences with words from 1.

1 Could you give me your email .... so that I can .... you an email?
2 My inbox is full. I need to .... some emails.
3 I have sent him an email but I am still waiting for him to .... to it.
4 Didn't you receive her email? I still have it and will .... it to you.
5 If you type in the wrong address, the email will .... back.
6 I want to open a new email .... with a different provider.
7 I am looking for an Internet café. I need to .... my emails.

3 LISTENING ▶ 40 Listen to the three dialogues and match the situations (1–3) with the topics (a–c).

Situation 1   a   a punishment
Situation 2   b   a work related question
Situation 3   c   a social event

4 ▶ 40 Listen to the dialogues again and choose the best answers.

1 What was Belinda's problem?
   a   She couldn't open the email.
   b   She lost the email.
   c   She didn't receive the email.
2 What did Daniel do wrong?
   a   He forgot to send the email.
   b   He made a mistake when he sent the email.
   c   He didn't check his inbox.
3 What did Penny do wrong?
   a   She went online during a lesson.
   b   She phoned someone during the class.
   c   She was chatting too much during the lesson.

VOCABULARY EXTENSION

5 With new technology such as the Internet, we often use abbreviations to name things more easily and quickly. Find the full names in the box for the abbreviations below. Use your dictionary if necessary. You can use some words more than once.

> asked • compact • digital • disc • frequently
> global • identification • memory • message
> number • only • personal • positioning
> questions • read • service • short • system
> versatile • web • wide • world

1 WWW = *world wide web*
2 DVD = ...
3 CD-ROM = ...
4 SMS = ...
5 GPS = ...
6 FAQ = ...
7 PIN = ...

6 Match the abbreviations with the definitions.

1 a secret number you need to operate a mobile phone, or use a credit card ....
2 a disc that people usually use to watch films ....
3 typical questions that people ask on a website ....
4 a large collection of documents, pictures and sounds kept on computers in many different places and connected through the Internet ....
5 a disc that computers can read, containing text, image and sound ....
6 a system for finding exactly where you are in the world using satellites ....
7 a way of sending a text message to a mobile phone ....

Grammar in context

1 **Read the rule about the passive and decide if it's true or false.**

To change the tense in passive sentences, we change the past participle.

2 **Circle the correct alternative.**

1 I *am/was* sent a lot of advertising emails last night.
2 Thousands of silicon chips *are/are being* made at this very moment.
3 I *was already/have already been* caught using my phone in class.
4 The book *One Hundred Years of Solitude was/has been* written by Gabriel García Márquez in 1967.
5 Many useful things *have been/were* invented since the start of the 20th century.
6 Penny *has/is* always being told off in class.

3 **Complete the sentences with the correct passive form of the verbs given.**

1 The cartoon character Mickey Mouse .... (create) in 1928.
2 Look! The restaurant .... (rename). I wonder when that happened.
3 The film *Gone with the Wind* .... (make) in 1939.
4 The pictures .... (draw) in prehistoric times.
5 The criminal .... (follow) by the police right now.
6 The first cheap cars .... (produce) nearly 100 years ago in the US.
7 Quick! Your favourite singer .... (interview) on TV right now.

4 **Write passive sentences using the prompts below.**

1 The novel *Animal Farm*/write/by George Orwell in 1945.
2 The race/organise/by the school each year.
3 Dynamite/invent/by Alfred Nobel in the 19th century.
4 Cartoons/watch/by thousands of children around the world at the moment.
5 The FIFA World Cup/win/by Brazil several times since 1958.
6 The planet Uranus/find/by William Herschel in 1781.
7 The men's 100-metre world record/break/by Usain Bolt in August 2009.

5 **Read the rules about *have something done* and decide if they are True (T) or False (F).**

1 We use *have something done* in all tenses. T / F
2 We use *have* + object + past participle. T / F
3 We can't use both *get* and *have* in this type of sentence. T / F
4 We use this type of sentence to say that someone else does an action for us. T / F

6 **Complete the dialogues with the correct form of the verbs in brackets.**

1 A: Your hair looks nice.
   B: Thanks. I .... (it/cut) last week.
2 A: Your car is making a strange noise.
   B: I know. I'll .... (it/check) soon.
3 A: Where's your new laptop?
   B: I .... (it/fix) at the moment. It crashed yesterday!
4 A: You don't usually wear glasses, do you?
   B: I do now. I .... (my eyes/test) on Saturday and I have to wear glasses all the time now.

GRAMMAR CHALLENGE

7 **Find and correct eight mistakes in the email.**

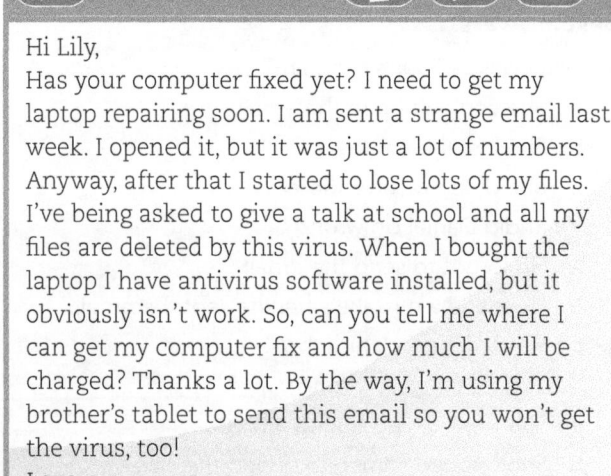

Hi Lily,
Has your computer fixed yet? I need to get my laptop repairing soon. I am sent a strange email last week. I opened it, but it was just a lot of numbers. Anyway, after that I started to lose lots of my files. I've being asked to give a talk at school and all my files are deleted by this virus. When I bought the laptop I have antivirus software installed, but it obviously isn't work. So, can you tell me where I can get my computer fix and how much I will be charged? Thanks a lot. By the way, I'm using my brother's tablet to send this email so you won't get the virus, too!
Love
Kim

Developing speaking

1 LISTENING ▶ 41 **Listen to a student comparing two photos. Complete her answer.**

OK, so yes, **(a)** .... of the pictures show people using computers, but they're using them in different places and for different reasons. In the first photo, the older people are looking at a computer together **(b)** ...., in the second photo the people have got their own computers. The older people look really happy and they're smiling. They're probably enjoying the activity. **(c)** ...., in the other photo the people are concentrating and they look very serious. I think they may be at a big meeting. **(d)** .... big difference is what the people are wearing. The older people are wearing casual clothes. In **(e)** ...., the people at the meeting are all wearing smart clothes. One **(f)** .... between the photos is that the computers are clearly important for the people. But apart from that they don't have a lot in **(g)** .... My grandparents were given a computer last year. They love it. My dad is a bit like the people in the **(h)** .... photo. He takes his computer to meetings all the time.

2 **Put the words in the correct order to find expressions to compare and contrast photos.**

1 photos of show the Both

....

2 similarity photos Another between important is the

....

3 they common Another in thing is have

....

4 between big photos difference is the One

....

5 other contrast people the In

....

PRONUNCIATION

3 ▶ 42 **Read the sentences and circle the /ð/ sounds and underline the /θ/ sounds. Listen and check.**

1 Another important thing is the location.
2 This weather is normal for this month.
3 These are my brother's clothes.
4 Thank you for your kind thoughts.
5 My teeth were checked on the third of June.
6 I threw away the dirty cloth yesterday.

DESCRIBING PICTURES

4 **Look at the photo and write your answers to the questions in your notebook. If you're not sure of something, use *I think* and/or *I imagine*.**

1 Who can you see in the photo?
2 Where are they?
3 What are they doing?
4 How do you think they are feeling? Why?

5 LISTENING ▶ 43 **Listen to a student talking about the photo. What are her answers to the questions?**

6 SPEAKING **Now look at the second photo and answer the same questions.**

STUDY SKILLS

What is the best way to improve your speaking?
➤ STUDY SKILLS page 95

Developing writing

1 The text message abbreviations for the words below are just one letter or number. Write the abbreviation for each one.

1. for ....
2. you ....
3. are ....
4. to/too ....
5. see ....
6. be ....

2 These text message abbreviations all use numbers. Think about how we pronounce the numbers and write the complete words with normal spelling.

1. 2day ....
2. 2nite ....
3. 2moro ....
4. B4 ....
5. L8 ....
6. GR8 ....
7. W8 ....
8. L8R ....

3 In these text message abbreviations some letters are missing or have been changed. Write the complete words with normal spelling.

1. YR ....
2. PLS ....
3. WOT ....
4. BCZ ....
5. SPK ....
6. WKND ....
7. THX ....
8. XLNT ....
9. MSG ....
10. HMWK ....

4 Write these text messages as complete sentences.

1. Can U PLS come 2 C me L8R?

2. I'll C U 2moro B4 school.

3. I'll W8 4 YR next MSG.

4. Wot R U doing at the WKND?

5. Will U B at home L8R 2day?

6. THX 4 the presents. They R GR8.

7. I can C U @ 6 BCZ I haven't got any HMWK.

5 Rewrite this conversation using text message abbreviations.

1. What are you doing tonight?

2. Amy and I are going to eat out because it's her birthday today. Do you want to come?

3. OK. Thanks. What time are you meeting?

4. At eight because before that I have to study for an exam tomorrow.

5. What time is your exam?

6. At ten. I have to go now. I'll speak to you later.

7. Great!

Revision: Units 1·2·3·4·5·6·7·8·9·10

Grammar

1 Rewrite the active sentences in the passive form and the passive sentences in the active form.

1. Grandparents play computer games, too.
   Computer games ....
2. Arthur Wynne invented crosswords in 1913.
   Crosswords ....
3. A museum is being opened by the Queen tomorrow.
   The Queen ....
4. The concert was seen by 40,000 people.
   40,000 people ....
5. Alex Smith has won the competition.
   The competition ....
6. They design Honda motorbikes in Japan.
   Honda motorbikes ....

2 Complete the sentences with the correct form of the verbs given.

1. I .... (tell) Eva if I .... (see) her this evening.
2. Mark said he .... (help) me with the project later that afternoon.
3. If I .... (be) the Prime Minister, I .... (build) more hospitals.
4. Yesterday I .... (have) an accident while I .... (play) tennis.
5. Emma .... (come) to the party, but she .... (not decide) yet.
6. .... (surf) the Net is my favourite hobby.
7. I enjoyed the film because I .... (not see) anything like it before.

3 Complete the text with the correct words.

My parents gave me **(a)** .... new tablet computer for my birthday and it **(b)** .... become my favourite gadget! I take it with me everywhere **(c)** .... I go. It's **(d)** .... lighter than my previous laptop and it's small **(e)** .... to put in my bag. I often use it on the train to read e-books or **(f)** .... emails. I also enjoy **(g)** .... TV and films on it. It's **(h)** .... best present I've ever had!

Vocabulary

1 Match words from the columns to make words connected to computers. Some words may match with more than one word.

1	key	....	a	engine
2	mouse	....	b	band
3	flash	....	c	board
4	hard	....	d	port
5	social	....	e	page
6	pass	....	f	mat
7	home	....	g	networking
8	search	....	h	drive
9	USB	....	i	copy
10	broad	....	j	word

2 Complete the sentences with the correct verbs.

1. Don't forget to .... off when you're finished so that I can use the laptop.
2. I like to .... online to my friends.
3. Dan sent me a good joke – I'll .... it to you.
4. If you .... on this link, you go to the website.
5. I usually .... a hard copy of my essays when I've typed them.

3 Complete the text with the words in the box.

address • bounces • delete • receive • reply • send

First find out the email **(a)** .... of the person you are writing to. Write the email, then **(b)** .... it. When you **(c)** .... an email, **(d)** .... to it quite quickly. When you have a lot of old emails, **(e)** .... them if you don't want to keep them. If an email **(f)** .... back, it's probably because you made a mistake.

4 Complete the sentences with prepositions.

1. I didn't switch .... the TV until 11.30 last night.
2. If you come .... my notes, don't throw them away!
3. I think it's important for friends to have some interests .... common.
4. I need to find .... when the concert starts.
5. I think Miles and Gina have fallen .... – they're not speaking to each other.
6. The teacher told us to turn .... the page.
7. I was flicking .... the book and I found this photo.

Gateway to exams: Units 9–10

Reading

1 Read the text. Put these sentences in the correct place. There is one extra sentence that you do not need.

a Does that mean that books are just a waste of our time?
b But these stories allow children to meet their own fears – in a perfectly safe and protected environment.
c The only answer I have ever been able to give is: because you have to.
d That is because stories are needed in our lives.
e Because I started my career as an author when I was just an adolescent.

Listening

2 LISTENING 44 Listen to the dialogues and complete the notes. You can write a maximum of three words and/or numbers.

Notepad

1 Tony is going to buy Sally a .... novel.
Tony usually does his book shopping ....

2 Ben had problems with his project because he didn't have .... at the beginning.
Ben had had problems with his .... connection.

3 In Lucy's crime novel, a .... is the detective.
Kay would like .... the crime novel from Lucy too.

4 Tom has decided that he .... his old phone.
Kathy told Tom that the new mobile phone is .... use.

The need for stories

At a Book Award ceremony author Paul Auster gave this speech. He was asked why he became a writer. This is what he said about it.

"I don't know why I do what I do. If I did know, I probably wouldn't feel the need to do it. All I can say is that I have needed to write stories since my earliest adolescence. It is an unusual way to spend your life – sitting alone in a room with a pen in your hand, hour after hour, day after day, year after year, trying to put words on pieces of paper in order to give birth to what does not exist – except in your own head. Why would anyone want to do such a thing? **(1)** .... This need to make, to create, to invent is essential for humans.

But fiction has no practical use in the real world. A book has never put food in the stomach of a hungry child. No bombs have ever been prevented from falling on innocent people in the middle of a war by a book.

In other words, art is no use when you compare it, for example, to the work of a doctor or an engineer. But ask yourselves if that is a bad thing. **(2)** .... Many people think so. But I would say that art is what makes us different from anything else on this planet. It is what defines us as human beings.

Children love listening to stories. Why? Fairy tales are often cruel and violent. You would think this would be too frightening for a young child. **(3)** .... This is the magic of stories.

For years, in every country of the western world, experts have told us that fewer and fewer people are reading books. This may be true, but at the same time this has not stopped the universal need for stories. Films and television and even comic books are creating vast quantities of narratives, and the public continues to read them with great passion. **(4)** .... It would be impossible to imagine life without them."

Use of English

3 Rewrite the sentences keeping the same meaning. Do not change the word given. Use between three and five words, including the word given.

1 'Where have you been, Jenny?' said Mr Judd.
she
Mr Judd asked ....

2 The mechanic checked my car for me yesterday.
had
I ....
the mechanic yesterday.

3 'You don't have to do Exercise 3,' said Miss Barnes.
us
Miss Barnes ....
not have to do Exercise 3.

4 Someone found my bag by the river this morning.
was
My ....
by the river this morning.

5 'Do you like your new tablet computer?' asked Jim.
me
Jim asked ....
new tablet computer.

6 They're interviewing the actor on TV at the moment.
is
The actor ....
on TV at the moment.

Writing

4 Your teacher has asked you to write a story. This is the title for it:

A computer saved my life.

Write the story.

COMMON MISTAKES

5 Correct the mistakes in the sentences. In some sentences there is more than one mistake.

1 Gemma said me that she had enjoyed the story.

2 The video clip was seen for millions of people last year.

3 My dad had built a wall in the garden by a local builder.

4 Jack said he will phone me the next day but he didn't.

5 This car is been made in Italy.

6 The waiter asked did we want any ice cream.

7 Both of pictures show people working in offices.

8 I'd like to start with saying that it's good to be here.

9 The criminal arrested the police yesterday.

10 The teacher told what would we do in the next lesson.

11 Lastly but not least, I'd like to talk about how much these products cost.

12 On the first photograph the sun is shining, but on the second it's raining hard.

Study skills

Unit 1

GRAMMAR: USING THE GRAMMAR REFERENCE
- When you have a problem with grammar, use reference material to find help.
- In the Student's Book there are grammar explanations on the Language Checkpoint pages at the end of each unit. These explanations help you to understand the correct use of the grammar (when and why to use the grammatical structure) and also the form (the correct parts of the structure).
- You can also use grammar books, either in English or in your own language.
- Internet websites can also provide help with typical grammar problems.

WRITING: KEEPING A MISTAKES CHECKLIST
It is normal to make mistakes when you write. That is why it is important to read your work carefully when you finish. Check for mistakes with:
- punctuation
- capital letters
- word order
- spelling
- tenses
- vocabulary
- missing words
- agreement between the subject and verb.

You can learn from your mistakes. Make a list of mistakes that you make with the correction next to it. Use it as a checklist when you are checking your writing. Look at this example.

Mistake	Correction	Explanation
In general, I think the money is important.	In general, I think money is important.	When we talk about things in general, we do not use the definite article.

Unit 3

KNOWING WHAT TYPE OF LEARNER YOU ARE
It is useful to know what type of learner you are because it can help you to improve. Here are some things to think about:
- Some people like working alone. But remember that language is usually a question of communication and working with a partner can be a great way to start communicating in English.
- Writing usually gives you time to think and prepare your message. But writing also needs to be very precise and correct.
- Speaking is quick and spontaneous. So when you speak, mistakes are normal. The important thing is that other people understand you.
- Mistakes are an essential part of learning a language. We can learn a lot from our mistakes.
- Some people don't like learning grammar, but grammar and vocabulary are the basic ingredients of any language. They help you to communicate.
- You can improve your memory. In general, we learn more with short, frequent revision.

LISTENING: KEEPING CALM
The worst thing that you can do when listening to English is panic because you don't understand something. It isn't usually necessary to understand every word. There is often repetition, and there are words that you don't need to understand to be able to do the activity. Concentrate on the information you need to answer the questions.

Unit 2

READING: PREDICTION
Before you read a text, look at the pictures or photos that go with it. Read the title of the text, too. This can help you to think about the topic of the text and to predict some of the ideas and words in it. It will help you to understand more when you read the text for the first time.

VOCABULARY: USING A DICTIONARY
Dictionaries are very useful. Here are some ideas for using them well:
- You can't always have a dictionary with you, for example, in exams. Don't depend on the dictionary too much. First, guess the word and then use your dictionary to check.
- When you are reading, don't use the dictionary to look up every word you don't know. You don't need to understand every word in a text to do the exercises or to understand the general meaning. Only look for words which appear important or appear frequently.
- Don't just look at the first definition for a word. Many English words have very different meanings. Look at them all and choose the right one for your context.
- Don't just think about the meaning of the word that you look up. Think also about the type of word, the form and spelling of the word, and the other words it often goes with.

Unit 4

VOCABULARY: KEEPING VOCABULARY RECORDS
To learn vocabulary, it is essential to keep a record of new words.
- Write down the meaning of new words. You can write a synonym, a definition, an example sentence, a translation, or you can draw a picture.
- It is also important to write down the type of word (e.g. noun, verb, adjective, adverb, preposition, pronoun) and any other special information (e.g. pronunciation, irregular forms).
- Some people write down new vocabulary using diagrams like this:

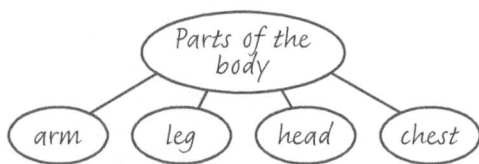

SPEAKING: WORDS YOU DON'T KNOW
When you don't know a word, don't stop and use a word in your own language. Here are some things you *can* do, using the word *freedom* as an example:
- use a synonym or similar word like *liberty* or *independence*
- use a more basic or general word or expression, *being free*
- say *It's the opposite of*, e.g. *It's the opposite of captivity*.
- explain the word using different words, e.g. *It's when you can do what you want.*

Unit 5

READING: READING FOR GENERAL INFORMATION
The first time you read a text, read it quickly. Do not stop if there are words you do not understand. Just try to understand the general meaning. Give yourself a time limit. It can help you to get a general understanding and not look at details. Look for specific information the second time you read.

GRAMMAR: USE AND FORM
When we study grammar we need to think about two basic things:
- we need to know the meaning and when to *use* the structure. For example, with *too* we need to know that we use it to talk about people, things or actions that are *excessive*.
- we need to know the *form* (including spelling). For example, we need to know that the word *too* comes before adjectives. Remember to think about both use and form when you do grammar activities.

Unit 6

LISTENING: FIRST LISTENING, SECOND LISTENING
- The first time you listen to a new text, the idea is to understand the general meaning, not to understand all the details. The first listening activity will usually help you to do this by asking general questions.
- The second time you listen you will need to listen for more specific information.

WRITING: ORGANISING IDEAS INTO PARAGRAPHS
- A paragraph is a number of sentences which talk about one or two main ideas. When you want to start to talk about a new main idea, you start a new paragraph. Paragraphs make your writing clear, organised and easy to understand.
- Before you start a piece of writing, make a note of the ideas that you want to include. Then put your ideas in a logical order and organise them into paragraphs.

Unit 7

VOCABULARY: EFFICIENT VOCABULARY REVISION
- Frequent revision is the best way to learn new words. Look at your vocabulary notebook or list every week and test yourself to see how much you remember. It is very difficult to learn vocabulary by revising just once before an exam or test.
- It is easier to learn vocabulary in groups, e.g. parts of the body, crimes, or adjectives ending in *-ing* and *-ed*. One word in a group can help you remember others in the same group.

SPEAKING: MAKING MISTAKES
- When you speak in a different language it is normal to make mistakes. The most important thing is to communicate with your partner.
- If you make small mistakes, either correct them when you make them or remember to work on them later.
- Remember: mistakes are a natural part of learning. If you don't say anything, you will never get better.

Unit 8

READING: READING FOR SPECIFIC INFORMATION
The first reading activity usually checks that you understand the general meaning of the text. The next activities check that you understand specific information. When you read for specific information, read the question carefully and then find the exact place where you think the answer comes.

LISTENING: LISTENING OUTSIDE THE CLASSROOM
The best way to improve your listening is by listening to as much English as possible. Apart from listening in class, try to listen to:
- CDs or audio files that come with books or readers
- original version films
- DVDs in English (with or without subtitles)
- the radio or Internet radio.

Unit 9

READING: READING FOR PLEASURE
Usually reading for pleasure means reading a whole book, magazine or website because you want to read it. There will probably be many words that you do not understand. It is not a good idea to stop every time you see a new word because you will never finish the story/article and you probably won't enjoy reading it. Only look up words that appear to be essential to understand the text, and that appear again and again. The main idea is to understand the general meaning … and to enjoy reading!

WRITING: PRACTISING YOUR WRITING
The best way to practise writing in English is to have an e-pal to write to who is English or who is another nationality to you but who can communicate in English. You can also go online and post comments on people's websites and blogs and reply to threads. Also, instead of phoning people why don't you send them instant messages in English?

Unit 10

READING: GUESSING FROM CONTEXT
You cannot usually use dictionaries in reading exams so when there are words that you do not understand, look carefully at the context to help you to guess the meaning. Look at the sentences and words just before and after the word. This can help you to find out the type of word (noun, verb, adjective, etc.) and the meaning.

SPEAKING: PRACTICE MAKES PERFECT
Speaking English is like riding a bike or playing tennis. You can only get better if you actually do it. The more you speak, the better you get. Speak as much English as possible in class, and outside the class.

Macmillan Education Limited
4 Crinan Street
London N1 9XW
A division of Macmillan Education Limited

Companies and representatives throughout the world

ISBN 978-0-230-47091-0

Text, design and illustration © Macmillan Education Limited 2016
Written by David Spencer and Lynda Edwards

The authors have asserted their right to be identified as the authors of this work in accordance with the Copyright, Designs and Patents Act 1988.

This edition published 2016
First edition entitled Gateway B1 Workbook published 2011 by Macmillan Education, S.A. de C.V.

All rights reserved. No part of this publication may be reproduced, stored in a retrieval system, transmitted in any form or by any means, electronic, mechanical, photocopying, recording, or otherwise, without the prior written permission of the publishers.

Designed by emc design ltd
Illustrated by A Corazon Abierto (Sylvie Poggio Artists Agency) pp30, 43, 50, 66; Monica Auriemma (Sylvie Poggio Artists Agency) pp16, 40, 42, 82; John Batten (Beehive Illustration) pp22, 24, 37, 48, 76; Tim Bradford (Illustration Ltd) pp51, 60.
Cover design by emc design ltd and Macmillan Education Limited
Cover illustration/photograph by Getty Images/Valentin Casarsa, Getty Images/Leonardo Patriz
Picture research by Emily Taylor

The publishers would like to thank the staff and pupils at the following schools in Mexico and Spain for helping us so enthusiastically with our research for the course:
Concha Campos, IES Burgo de Las Rozas, Las Rozas, Madrid; Félix Gaspar, IES Las Encinas; Villanueva de la Cañada, Madrid; Cristina Moisen, IES Joaquín Turina, Madrid; Colegio Montessori Cuautitlán; Colegio Conrad Gessner; Colegio Erasmo de Rotterdam; Colegio Kanic, Centro Educativo Erich Fromm; Universidad Franco Mexicana; Centro Pedagógico María Montessori de Ecatepec; Instituto Cultural; Escuela Maestro Manuel Acosta; Liceo Sakbé De México.

The publishers would also like to thank all those who reviewed or piloted the first edition of Gateway:
Benjamin Affolter, Evelyn Andorfer, Anna Ciereszynska, Regina Culver, Anna Dabrowska, Justyna Deja, Ondrej Dosedel, Lisa Durham, Dagmar Eder, Eva Ellederovan, H Fouad, Sabrina Funes, Luiza Gervescu, Isabel González Bueno, Jutta Habringer, Stela Halmageanu, Marta Hilgier, Andrea Hutterer, Nicole Ioakimidis, Mag. Annemarie Kammerhofer, Irina Kondrasheva, Sonja Lengauer, Gabriela Liptakova, Andrea Littlewood, María Cristina Maggi, Silvia Miranda Barbara Nowak, Agnieszka Orlińska, Anna Orlowska, María Paula Palou, Marta Piotrowska, N Reda, Katharina Schatz, Roswitha Schwarz, Barbara Ścibor, Katarzyna Sochacka, Joanna Spoz, Monica Srtygner, Marisol Suppan, Stephanie Sutter, Halina Tyliba, Prilipko, Maria Vizgina, Vladyko, Pia Wimmer, Katarzyna Zadrożna-Attia and Katarzyna Zaremba-Jaworska.

The author and publishers would like to thank the following for permission to reproduce their photographs.
Alamy/Allstar Picture Library p26, Alamy/BSIP SA p33(3); **The British Library** © The British Library Board, C:105.f.3, p.opp18 p81(tl); **Corbis** p27(tr), Corbis/2/Winston Davidian/Ocean p58(6), Corbis/2/Nick White/Ocean p89(cl), Corbis/Bettman Archive p14, Corbis/B. Boissonnet/BSIP p33(5), Corbis/Phil Boorman p20(tl), Corbis/Matt Dutile p52, Corbis/Kai Foersterling/epa p85(tr), Corbis/Fotofeeling/Westend61 p56(tl), Corbis/Don Mason/Blend Images p17(br), Corbis/Toby Melville/Reuters p49, Getty Images/Michael Ochs Archives p23, Corbis/Moodboard p35(tr), Corbis/The Star Ledger p8(tr), Corbis/Mel Stuart/Westend61 p30; **Getty Images**/Daniel Berehulak p74, Getty Images/Blend Images pp77, 81(br), Getty Images/Bloom Productions p18, Getty Images/Blue Jean Images p33(1), Getty Images/Brand X p17(tr), Getty Images/Dario Cantatore p92(tl), Getty Images/Damircudic p89(cr), Getty Images/Dominique Charriau p56(br), Getty Images/Diana Hirsch p58(5), Getty Images/Juanmonino p31, Getty Images/Diane Labombarbe p64, Getty Images/Rich Legg p36, Getty Images/Kristian Sekulic pp45(br), 72, Getty Images/StockByte p20(tr), Getty Images/Sturtic p41, Getty Images/Klaus Vedfelt p71(tr), Getty Images/Westend61 p28, Getty Images/Yellow Dog Productions p81(tr); **Sarah Kaufmann**/Image courtesy of Sarah Kaufmann p59; **The Picture Desk**/The Kobal Collection/ABC-TV p33(tr), The Picture Desk/The Kobal Collection/Translux p46; **PlainPicture**/wuppclupp p5; **Rex Features**/ITV pp13(tl, tr), 15; **ThinkStock** p54, ThinkStock/Keith Brofsky p58(bl), ThinkStock/Digital Vision p9(br), ThinkStock/Getty Images/F1online RF p53(tr), ThinkStock/Getty Images/Fuse p27(br), 70, ThinkStock/Getty Images/Huntstock p45(tr), ThinkStock/Getty Images/iStockphoto pp8(bl), 9(mr), 33(4), 33(6), 35(br), 53(br), 58(2,3,4), 67, 71(br), 85(hands typing), 89(tl,br), 90, 92(br), ThinkStock/Getty Images/moodboard RF p58(1), ThinkStock/Getty Images/Wavebreak Media pp35(tl), 85(background code), ThinkStock/iStock Images/lisafx p25, ThinkStock/Monkey Business Images Ltd p33(2), ThinkStock/Photodisc p63(br); **The Wellcome Library,** London p38(a,b,c).

These materials may contain links for third party websites. We have no control over, and are not responsible for, the contents of such third party websites. Please use care when accessing them.

Printed and bound by CPI Group (UK) Ltd, Croydon, CR0 4YY

POD 2025